3 9082 12131 3095

T 368.1 H [Careers]

D1367785

Career Launcher

Health Care Management

Career Launcher series

Career Launcher

Health Care Management

Marcia Horowitz

Ferguson Publishing
An imprint of Infobase Publishing

Career Launcher: **Health Care Management**

Ferguson
An imprint of Infobase Publishing
132 West 31st Street
New York NY 10001

Library of Congress Cataloging-in-Publication Data

Horowitz, Marcia.
  Health care management / by Marcia Horowitz.
    p. ; cm. — (Career launcher)
  Includes bibliographical references and index.
  ISBN-13: 978-0-8160-7969-8 (hardcover : alk. paper)
  ISBN-10: 0-8160-7969-2 (hardcover : alk. paper)
1. Health services administration. I. Title. II. Series: Career launcher.
  [DNLM: 1. Health Services Administration—United States.
2. Administrative Personnel—United States.
3. Vocational Guidance—United States. W 84 AA1 H813h 2009]
  RA971.H578 2009
  362.1068—dc22

                                                      200904979

Ferguson books are available at special discounts when purchased in bulk quantities for businesses, associations, institutions, or sales promotions. Please call our Special Sales Department in New York at (212) 967-8800 or (800) 322-8755.

You can find Ferguson on the World Wide Web at http://www.fergpubco.com

Produced by Print Matters, Inc.
Text design by A Good Thing, Inc.
Cover design by Takeshi Takahashi
Cover printed by Art Print Company, Taylor, PA
Book printed and bound by Maple Press, York, PA
Date printed: August 2010

Printed in the United States of America

10 9 8 7 6 5 4 3 2 1

This book is printed on acid-free paper.

Contents

Foreword

For the past five years, I have been president and CEO of a large health care system that includes hospitals, physician group practices, many outpatient entities, and 7,500 employees. This certainly was not my goal when I went off to college to become a music major! In speaking to my colleagues who run similar health care organizations, I find that we come from varied backgrounds and few of us foresaw what we would eventually end up doing. My story involves a degree in pharmacy, several years of work inside a hospital environment, subsequent graduate school, and then several positions that evolved into my current opportunity. Some of my colleagues have come through clinical backgrounds, finance backgrounds, or various other experiences that helped prepare them for a career in health care management.

Some of you may start out, as I did, in smaller facilities, and graduate to more senior-level jobs in larger ones. There are many issues and challenges that are similar to both—but there are differences in running a large health care organization. For one, as with other businesses, there are all of the inherent leadership challenges. One has to be skilled in all aspects of human resource management, leadership, relationship-building, developing a team of leaders, and ensuring that the team has the right talents to do the jobs. As with all businesses, there are the needs for strong analytical thinking, financial skills, and a strategic orientation. Also, there is a premium on execution—that is, holding people accountable, understanding the role information technology plays in our business, and having the ability to measure performance over time. All of the aforementioned are key competencies that are required for any business leader.

In health care, what is unique is that at the same time you are running this business, you also are dealing with people's lives. You are entering patient and family lives at a time when they are often most vulnerable, confused, and frightened. So, while there is a high value for the basic business skills, leadership in health care also requires the mission-driven focus that successful health care executives must exhibit.

The very challenges that make a large health care enterprise different from a normal business enterprise are also some of the rewards that come with being a health care leader. You realize that you are working for the greater good and that you are able to offer something more than just a business proposition to patients and to your community. You have the opportunities to work with individuals at all types of jobs and levels and to create unique teams of individuals from across many different skill and professional areas. You are able to see how your work really does impact people's lives. You come to work every day knowing that it is going to be different than the day before, and that the challenges of tomorrow will be different from those that you have seen previously in your career.

So, how do you successfully find a place in this field? You need to understand the demands of leadership—all of those characteristics mentioned above—and all the skills that you need in leading any organization. This means mastering the financial wherewithal, the human resource skills, the leadership skills, and the strategic-thinking skills required in the business world. But, you must also be grounded in the needs of the patients and the communities that you serve, and how the delivery system in which you work is structured to meet those needs. Health care also functions within an overall regulatory system, which is unique to every field of industry, and a leader needs to understand the requirements and the complexities involved.

Once you have received some of the basic background required, and perhaps even have your first position within a health care organization, where do you seek the information about how to become even more successful? I have found that most individuals in health care are pleased to be asked to help others, to mentor them, and to point them to good information sources regarding health care and future opportunities. It is a very complex system and field, and in order to map a career one must be willing to consult books, industry periodicals, and professional organizations.

A few questions I would be asking were I starting out or transferring into a career in this field are: 1) What are the important organizations that influence how the industry is defined? 2) What are wage scales and job outlooks for hospital administrators? (This is perhaps an area that was key to me, but you may be looking at opportunities in finance, human resources, marketing, consulting, or others.) 3) How did the industry get started, and what influences and events caused it to evolve into the form that it has today? 4) What would someone who has been in the field and who is experienced tell you about how to succeed in it?

Whether you are experienced in health care leadership, just starting out and looking to make it a lifelong career, or coming from a different professional field entirely, I applaud you for your interest. I know that the opportunity to be challenged each and every day has been extremely rewarding. I know that when I reach the end of my career, I will leave with the satisfaction of not only having had a personally rewarding position, but also knowing that I have had the opportunity to help my fellow man.

—Tim Rice
President and CEO
Moses Cone Health System
Greensboro, North Carolina

Acknowledgments

Writing this book would not have been possible without the invaluable contributions from the dedicated health care management professionals who provided me with interviews. They helped me understand the field and the people who work in it. I am most grateful for the wisdom and the knowledge of:
Dr. Oscar Aylor, Director of Mercy Ministries, Mission to the World, Atlanta, Georgia. Robert Goldstein, FACMPE, Executive Vice President, Physician Network, Moses Cone Health System, and Vice President, LeBauer Health Care, Greensboro, North Carolina. Joel Mills, Chief Executive Officer, Advanced Home Care, High Point, North Carolina. Tim Rice, President and CEO of Moses Cone Health System, Greensboro, North Carolina. Cynthia Robinson, Manager, Healthcare Practice Consultants at Davenport, Martin, Joyce & Co., LLP, Greensboro, North Carolina.

Finding just the right information was facilitated by the astute librarians at the Greensboro Public Library, the High Point Public Library, and the Walter C. Jackson Library at the University of North Carolina at Greensboro. I thank all of you for having the specialized knowledge to point me in the right direction.

Finally, to my husband Lee who put up with the clicking away in the office upstairs for many a day and night—thanks for plying me with caffeine and encouragement when the inspiration flagged.

Introduction

Much of what you will find in this book relates to a prediction, a fact, and a surprise.

Here is the prediction: If you continue to pursue a career in the field of health care management, you can likely depend on a steady, constantly growing, lucrative, and satisfying career. Of course, no one can predict the future, but all the signs point to the field expanding at a rapid rate—even with the fluctuations in the economy and with impending changes to the health care system. The need for people to occupy health care administration jobs will be with us when other careers decline.

This is because of several factors. The population keeps growing and at the same time getting older, necessitating the establishment of more and more health care facilities to care for them. As the need expands so do hospitals, private practices, clinics, research facilities, academic programs, public health services, and other venues where administrators are needed. Moreover, with the passage of health care legislation by Congress, estimates are that the 45 million or so individuals who are now without insurance will enter the system via a form of a public option.

The opportunity is evident. The most recent information from the Bureau of Labor Statistics reveals that the medical and health service management industries employed over a quarter of a million people in 2006 and that "[e]mployment of medical and health services managers is expected to grow 16 percent from 2006 to 2016, faster than average, for all occupations." Even with cost cutting, salaries in the field are increasing and a multitude of career opportunities exist and will continue to for years to come.

And, here is the fact: There is a variety of health care administration jobs in many settings. Health care administrators are not just hospital presidents, as some might imagine. Administrators can be found in medical clinics, consulting firms, health insurance organizations, physician practices, mental health organizations, public health departments, rehabilitation centers, skilled nursing facilities, universities and research institutes, and in all branches of the military. They can be generalists in health management or in a specialized area such as finance, government relations, human resources, information technology, marketing and public relations, materials management, nursing administration, medical staff relations, patient care services, fund-raising, and planning and development. The many settings provide great opportunity for career flexibility in the field.

And now the surprise: Not everybody who is a health care manager now intended it as a career. In fact, it is often called a "hidden" career because many job-seekers are not aware of it or have difficulty in finding career resources that relate to it. There are some surprising career paths. You will read how several of the interviewees for this book set their sights on another career and sort of "fell into" health care management—with happy results. Bob Goldstein wanted to be a doctor, but he ran into a fraternity brother who "told me that there was a field that a lot of people did not know about called health administration." Bob got a master's degree in health administration at Duke University and has occupied senior positions in several medical practices. But he admits that "my kids still do not know what I do. People still do not know how you get to be a hospital administrator." Others developed in the field through deliberate decisions to incorporate their own personal values in their work. Joel Mills, who majored in history but eventually found a career as CEO of a home health care company, says this on values: "I believe that one of the keys to success in health care management is to have seen it at the patient-care level—the caring spirit of support." Tim Rice, president and CEO of a large hospital system, who started as a music major, became a pharmacist, and ultimately transitioned into health administration says, "People come to us in times of need and fear. I get enjoyment out of making the patient experience a positive one by trying to manage how well they are treated. This career is very rewarding."

Key Goals

The key goal for the book is to give you the most important and most current information on careers in health care administration so that you will have a leg-up as you advance to the next level. If you have ever asked the question, "What exactly is it that health care managers do and how do they do it?" you are familiar with the limitations of information about the field. Although some career guides address the tasks of the general health manager and others describe particular specialties, this information is often lumped in with facts about clinical health careers. What is harder to find is a separate and distinct comprehensive guide on health care management careers that really fleshes out the landscape of job variety, settings, career paths, resources, and advice from seasoned professionals.

This book aims to be a complete and easy-to-use guide that saves the job-seeker many hours of job-research time. In it you will find the most salient information about career entry and career success in an easy-to-use format that facilitates finding the answers to your questions.

The book also strives to define the scope and range of the field in order to help you determine what career areas are suitable and interesting to you. If you are on the cusp of deciding whether to take that hospital marketing job or that nursing home administrator's job, the Web sites in the resource section, the capsules that detail the job requirements, and the advice from experts in the field can help with the decision.

Finally, a primary goal of the book is to give the reader a real inside view of the workings of health care management jobs. Going beyond descriptions, the stories and interviews lay bare what the administrator might encounter in a day's work—the satisfactions and the pitfalls. You will see up close the response of Joel Mills, a CEO of a home care company, when asked what it takes to succeed in this field. Oscar Aylor speaks of the challenges and rewards of an academic career.

Your Friend in the Business: Using This Book

This book assumes that you already have some knowledge of the field or are already in it. It will be your friend in the business by giving you the tools you need to hit the ground running in your job search or as you navigate the terrain of a new job. But before you sit down and open to the first chapter, think about where you are now in your life or your career, and then picture where you want to be. Perhaps you have just acquired an undergraduate or graduate degree in health care administration and are looking at graduate programs. You could be in an entry-level position in a health care setting and looking to move up. Or you could be a marketing executive, a financial staffer, or a clinical professional looking to transfer those skills into the health care management field. To find answers to the questions that accompany any of these scenarios, this book can be read sequentially to give you the entire scope of the industry, or you can use the chapters individually to get a better understanding of one or two aspects of the field you would like to know more about.

For instance, if you want to know the variety of jobs in the field and the experience needed for them, the "On the Job" chapter contains specific capsules that succinctly describe the "feel" of the job, where they are commonly located, what experience and schooling is needed, what the typical tasks are, and many other useful facts. Or if you want to better understand the language and terminology of the profession—useful to have when you are on an interview—turn to the "Talk Like A Pro" chapter. All of the chapters are constructed to answer your most pressing questions about entering and sustaining a career within the field.

Moreover, several well-established professionals were interviewed for this book, and their words convey experience and guidance. They demonstrate the decision-making processes involved in advancing in the field and the struggles and successes that followed. These interviews often address the below-the-radar questions that pop up in any career-research effort.

The Research Process

Research for this book consisted of consulting relevant career guides and books, articles, professional organizations, and Web sites. The research also focused on examining the latest and most targeted information from the Bureau of Labor Statistics, the American College of Healthcare Executives, the Medical Group Management Association, Women in Healthcare Management, and the Healthcare Financial Management Association. Invaluable to this process and the final product are the interviews that were conducted with established professionals in the field.

What Is In This Book?

This book is organized into six chapters: "Industry History," "State of the Industry," "On the Job," "Tips for Success," "Talk Like a Pro," and "Resources."

The "Industry History" chapter facilitates understanding on how health care management traditions and practices emerged and what they are like today. It also provides insight into how the major organizations that drive the industry first formed and what makes the industry tick. A short chronology that highlights crucial dates and events underscores the industry's rich traditions and story. Dr. Oscar

Aylor, a former professor of health policy and administration, provides an expert view on how the industry has been shaped by its past.

For a detailed understanding of the current state of health care management in the United States, the "State of the Industry" chapter provides statistics on employment, wages, profits, and current and future trends. It also provides important information on new technology in the field, key conferences and industry events, major organizations and companies in the field, issues of law and government—like the most recent legislation on the operation of health care facilities—and personal insights about opportunities in the industry. Bob Goldstein, vice-president of a large group practice, gives us informed insights on current and future trends and on other issues.

Because the scope of jobs is so large, the "On the Job" chapter provides separate job-description capsules in six occupational areas. Each capsule describes what role the job serves within an organization, the demands of the job, the career path often taken to get the job, educational requirements, and salary ranges where available.

The "Tips for Success" chapter gives industry-specific advice for planning a career path in the industry, pointers on job-hunting and interviewing, and what it takes to succeed once you get the job. The interview with Joel Mills, CEO of a home health care company, provides an intimate view of daily tasks, events, and requirements that can help you form a better idea of the day-to-day rewards and challenges of the career.

The "Talk Like A Pro" section provides an extensive glossary of industry jargon and frequently used terms. It will help readers better understand the key terminology, phrases, concepts, and business language that are in play in health care management environments. Whether beginning in the field or moving up in it, readers will be able to walk into a new job familiar with language that will help shorten the learning curve.

Specialized training in health services administration is offered at both graduate and undergraduate levels, and information on these programs can be found in the "Resources" section, which includes comprehensive listings of training programs and professional organizations. Additionally, key books and periodicals from all the various areas of health administration, Web sites, and other resources provide access to the most current material needed to manage a career effectively.

"I Cannot Imagine Doing Anything Else"

During times of economic uncertainty, health care management is a field that provides an island of stability. There are indeed challenges, though, and many of the individuals quoted or interviewed for this book will tell you of many days that tried them and that working in the field is sometimes no bed of roses. Cynthia Robinson, a health care consultant who was interviewed for this book, advises that you have to be willing to do some jobs that no one else wants to do to get experience. But she also says about her more than 25-year career in health administration: "I cannot imagine doing anything else. Most people who do it enjoy it. It is a helping profession, and it is all about patient care."

Chapter 1

Industry History

The history of modern health care management is short. The institutions that administrators now run did not exist in large part before the end of the 19th century. Though brief and full of ups and downs, this history is nonetheless illuminating, as it shows how quickly the need for administrators became evident when the modern health care system began to emerge.

Hospitals: Where It All Started

Today we are accustomed to patronizing hospitals, medical centers, group practices, and clinics for our health needs in times of illness. But it was not always so. For most of the 19th century in the United States and long before that, most people were treated at home by doctors or were not treated at all. In the rest of the world, hospitals had existed in some form for centuries, but there were few hospitals in the original thirteen colonies. One of the first was the Pennsylvania Hospital established in Philadelphia in the mid-1700s by Benjamin Franklin and Dr. Thomas Bond. For the most part, hospitals were largely asylums for the indigent, and it was considered a death sentence to be quartered at one. The chances were slight of surviving in an institution full of people with communicable diseases and with medical staff who had little knowledge of infection control.

Beginning around 1870, the American hospital began to undergo a transformation that led to the modern institutions that we know today. Cynthia Haddock and her colleagues (2002), who are professors and professionals in the health care administration field, note the shift. They report that religious groups, industrial organizations, ethnic associations, women's groups, coteries of wealthy and influential individuals, and religious orders began establishing institutions where their constituents could go to be treated or to die in safe and relatively comfortable surroundings. The trend was spurred by population growth through immigration, especially in the larger cities. The growth of cities like Milwaukee and St. Louis was reflected in the large hospitals that were built there before the 20th century

Everyone
Knows

There are three basic types of hospitals in the United States: proprietary (for-profit) hospitals, nonprofit hospitals, and government-supported hospitals. The services within these institutions vary considerably, but are usually organized around the basic mission(s) or objective(s) of the institution.

- *Proprietary hospitals.* For-profit hospitals include both general and specialized hospitals, usually as part of a health care network like Humana or HCA, which may be corporately owned. The main objective of proprietary hospitals is to make a profit from the services provided.

- *Teaching or nonprofit hospitals.* These are hospitals that serve several purposes. They provide patients for the training or research of interns and residents, and they also offer services to patients who are unable to pay for services while attempting to maintain profitability. Nonprofit centers like the University of California at San Francisco (UCSF) or the Mayo Clinics combine service, teaching, and profitability without being owned by a corporation or private owner.

- *Government-supported hospitals.* This group includes tax-supported hospitals for counties, towns, and cities with nonprofit hospitals that are run by a board of citizen administrators who serve without pay. The main objective of this type of hospital is to provide health care for a community or geographic region.

dawned. Additionally, many small hospitals were established by individual physicians who needed places to care for patients following surgery and other medical procedures. Between 1875 and 1925, the number of hospitals in the United States grew from just over 170 to about 7,000.

In fact, the establishment of hospitals at this time became a national movement. The U.S. Census Bureau in its surveys in 1904 and again in 1910 considered the development of hospitals as a "public undertaking," providing a new kind of institution that was a model of technology, cleanliness, and efficiency. The noise, dirt, smell of festering wounds, and unruly patients of an earlier era were gone. In their place, there were drugs for pain relief, a concerted effort at understanding and managing disease, an air of discipline and tightly controlled hygienic practices, and a real sense that illness could be controlled. Rosemary Stevens (1989), who has written extensively on the history of American hospitals, describes the reaction of Henry James who had returned to America from Europe in 1905: "Presbyterian Hospital in New York and Johns Hopkins Hospital in Baltimore were symbols of stillness, whiteness, poetry, manners, and tone—necessary values, he considered, amidst the violence, vulgar materialism, and hurly-burly of America".

As time passed, more and more people considered hospitals as safe places for treatment and recovery. A real indicator of public trust occurred when babies began to be born in them. In 1929, less than 29 percent of all births took place in hospitals, but in 1940 that figure rose to 56 percent. Patients began to realize that hospitals were there for their benefit.

Early Health Care Administrators Come Into Their Own

In the first hospitals, administrators were called *superintendents*. Mostly they were nurses who had absorbed administrative responsibilities into their clinical duties. But the rapid growth in hospitals required a broader set of competencies from these new administrators, and there arose a need to communicate with others who were endeavoring to develop as health managers. By the 1890s, the first fledgling group of administrators organized and formed their own association called the Association of Hospital Superintendents. This group later morphed into what is now the American Hospital Association.

As hospitals became larger and more complex, the new norm was to run them like businesses, emphasizing a drive for efficiency. Physicians, nurses, and the newly minted hospital administrators felt that hospitals as complex institutions should be run like Henry Ford's well-functioning motorcar businesses. In the 1910s and 1920s, they would engage in what was in vogue at the time— *scientific management.* In this way of approaching hospital management, it was important to understand productivity—emphasizing the roles of measurement, standardization, performance, coordination of operations, and motivation of workers. Hospitals were encouraged to standardize their medical record-keeping and their financial reporting. As hospitals navigated a course toward better management, conflicts inevitably arose and administrators found themselves in new roles such as keeping the peace among physicians, boards, and private and public donors.

Administrators felt keenly the need to separate their function from that of the physician- or nurse-administrator, the model from earlier times. So, they began to acquire discrete areas of function within hospital settings: They centered their operations on housekeeping, accounting, public relations, fund-raising, and human resources issues, leaving the majority of patient-care concerns in the hands of clinical staff. A quiet agreement existed between the clinical and the administrative staffs that neither area would conflict, but rather that they would work in concert for the greater good of the institution.

A Focus on Social Welfare

In the early- to mid-20th century, another shift took place in the distribution of health care. With the development of more institutions created to provide medical attention, payment for services in those institutions became an issue. When hospitals became places where people felt safe in taking their health issues, they were patronized by those who could pay for the services out-of-pocket—essentially the rich and near-rich. However, when the Great Depression occurred in the 1930s, the federal government began to take a more active role in providing programs for all classes of citizens. Along with programs to get people back to work and to provide for the indigent, the government began to consider national health programs and ways to improve public health. Frances Perkins, Secretary of Labor under President Franklin Roosevelt and one of the creators of the New Deal policies, pushed a national health insurance program in the 1930s as part of the Social Security Act. There were a string of government interventions that set the stage for the more equitable distribution of care. Beaufort Longest and Kurt Darr (2008), who write extensively on health policy issues, suggest that the following initiatives in the mid-20th century were key:

➡ Although national health plans had been considered since the 1940s, it was not until the Medicare and Medicaid bills were passed in 1966 (as an amendment to the Social Security Act of 1935) that a segment of the population's health needs was covered by federal mandate. Medicare pays for medical services provided to persons who have disabilities or are age 65 or over. Medicaid is run by the states and is subsidized by the federal government. It offers a range of health services to participants who qualify—usually on an income basis.

➡ The Hill-Burton Act of 1946 provided more than $4 billion in grants and loans for the construction of hospitals and health facilities that contributed to the building of and assistance to nearly 6,900 hospitals in more than 4,000 communities. In exchange for this assistance, health organizations had to provide services for those unable to pay for varying lengths of time.

➡ The National Institutes of Health, which traces its roots back to 1887, began an aggressive program of research, especially on cancer. This has led to a level of government funding that in 2007 was $28.6 billion for research activities in universities, medical schools, and independent research institutions.

➡ In the 1960s, federal programs were established to train more physicians, nurses, technicians, and managers.

➡ Veterans Administration hospitals were built and institutions for health services were established for groups such as inmates in federal prisons, American Indian and Alaskan natives, and active-duty and retired military personnel and their dependents.

➡ Over the years, federal legislators have continued to legislate in favor of both containing costs and improving services—two goals that are sometimes in conflict with one another. Health care costs have increased dramatically as compared to costs for other services in the rest of the economy, and that has created a need for more efficient delivery.

A Struggle Ensues to Establish a New Field

As the 20th century progressed, health administrators not only adapted to the ever-widening context that was being created for their services, but also innovated by creating systems, institutions, policies, and best practices. But it was not easy. Turf issues and conflicts over setting standards soon took over.

An interesting turf issue is the one that occurred between the sexes. In 1916, graduate nurses made up half the membership of the American Hospital Association. In addition to nurses, a hospital superintendent could also be a physician, a layperson, or a Catholic sister. Eventually, women got pushed aside as this new niche was gradually occupied by men who perceived an opportunity in which they could be successful in the burgeoning economy of the early 20th century.

With the growth of health institutions taking place at such a rapid pace, administrators were running to catch up in terms of staffing and training. Added to that, there was little agreement over standards for the field. Large and small hospitals had different agendas and constituencies and were run accordingly. Also, those administrators who saw hospital care as an outgrowth of a vigorous public health agenda were rarely supported by their trustees. There were exceptions: for example, when the head of the Boston Dispensary with the support of the board and administrators started a pay clinic for middle-income workers in 1913 that supported personal and public health awareness. However, administrators in most settings lacked a common purpose and a sense of unity, which in those very early days inhibited the creation of a national organization for hospital administrators.

Development of the First Professional Organization and University Programs

Two areas of activity flourished during the 20th century that were critical in establishing the field. First, professional organizations began to be established to represent the people employed in the field and to set standards. Second, educational programs were developed to educate potential health care administrators. These initiatives helped to formulate the health care management infrastructure that exists today.

In 1933, a group of practicing administrators came together to form the American College of Hospital Administrators (now the American

College of Health Care Executives [ACHE]). The emphasis of the new group was on the lay administrator. Of the 106 charter fellows of the new association, 16 were women and 32 were physicians. Then in 1934, the University of Chicago established its first graduate program in hospital administration. The impetus for the program was a book by Michael Davis called *Hospital Administration, A Career: The Need for Trained Executives for a Billion Dollar Business, and How They May Be Trained*. Published in 1929, Davis's book proposed a two-year graduate degree curriculum in hospital administration that would cover the following subjects in the first year: accounting, statistics, management, economics and the social sciences, and the history of hospitals and the health professions. In the second year, there would be mostly practice work and some coursework in business policy, public health, and labor relations. Davis was ultimately named head of the new program in Chicago, which closely followed the model he proposed in the book.

What is significant about these two events is that hospital administration was finally becoming a field in its own right. This was recognized in 1932 at a meeting of the Committee on the Costs of Medical Care, where hospitals were defined as large, complex medical, social, and business institutions that needed to be directed by administrators who received high-level training in university programs or in institutes of hospital administration. It was a call for talented individuals who would regard hospital administration as a worthy and fulfilling career.

Fast
Facts
The First Hospital Administration Degrees

Although the first program in health economics was established in 1900 at Columbia Teachers' College for graduate nurses, it was quite a while before a formal degree-granting program in hospital administration was created. Father Moulinier of the Catholic Hospital Association developed one at Marquette University in Wisconsin, but by 1928 it had closed with only two women having received degrees.

After the Chicago program opened, eight new programs in hospital administration were established in the 1940s, nine more in the 1950s, and 15 more in the 1960s. These programs called their degree programs "hospital administration," but later the degree came to be titled "health care administration." This change reflected that students were anticipating working in a wider range of organizations and not just hospitals. As the decades passed, the field of health care administration came to encompass such settings as ambulatory care facilities, consulting firms, health care associations, home health agencies, hospices, hospitals and hospital systems, integrated delivery systems, long-term care facilities, managed care organizations (such as HMOs and PPOs), medical group practices, mental health organizations, public health departments, university or research institutions, and military health facilities.

Minorities and Women Enter the Field and Establish Professional Organizations

Although the first program in health economics was established in 1900 at Columbia Teachers' College for graduate nurses, it was quite a while before a formal degree-granting program in hospital administration was created. Women and minorities began to enter the field in the late 1920s when it became a separate career option distinct from the clinical side. As they came into the field in increasing numbers, their focus was often on the distinct needs of their identity groups. Eventually, women and minorities began to establish separate professional groups that would represent their views. One of these, the National Association of Health Services Executives (NAHSE) places its origin as far back as the early 1930s, when a group of African-American health executives formed what was then called the National Hospital Association (NHA), an affiliate of the National Medical Association (NMA).

In 1936, at a meeting at Lincoln Hospital in Durham, North Carolina, the NHA was renamed the National Conference of Hospital Administration (NCHA). After several changes in leadership, the Conference's activities were limited to one informal meeting held in conjunction with the annual AHA meeting. In 1968, NAHSE was formed for the purpose of promoting the advancement and development of African-American health care leaders, elevating the quality of health care services rendered to minority and underserved

Best Practice

Diversity in Health Care

Diversity is a top priority for most if not all health care institutions. But implementing the goal of providing a culturally competent and diverse workforce can be difficult without good planning. One major hospital system reached its diversity goals by instituting something called a "circuit breaker" wherein the incentive programs of all senior leaders relied on the completion of a three-year diversity and inclusion plan. If any part of the organization failed to develop a plan, no one in the management structure would have received his or her at-risk performance incentive pay. There was 100 percent participation.

communities, and having greater input in the national health care delivery system.

An organization called Women in Healthcare Management (WHCM) was founded in Boston, Massachusetts, to provide a forum for professional women to meet peers, network, share information, and stay informed on issues affecting the health care field. Its members are managers in settings and organizations spanning the wide range of the health care industry. WHCM services include two large group meetings annually, periodic networking meetings, a job bank, inclusion in the annual member directory, and the opportunity to form small groups for more frequent and informal networking.

The Association of Hispanic Health care Executives (AHHE) was founded in 1988 as a national voluntary organization seeking to foster programs and policies to increase the presence of Hispanics in health administration professions. AHHE is the first organization devoted exclusively to Hispanic health care executives and to the education of the health care industry about the Hispanic health care marketplace.

The Asian Health Care Leaders Association (ASHCLA) is a membership and leadership organization devoted to increasing the representation and professional development of Asian-Americans in health care executive management, policy, and administration.

The organization has programs in mentoring, networking, lifelong learning, and career development that are designed to serve individuals and organizations at all levels and across all disciplines of the health care field and serves as a networking point for Asian-Americans in clinical fields who may be interested in moving into leadership roles.

Administrators and Physicians: Two Different Perspectives

Hospital administrators began to assert themselves, especially in the large, urban hospital systems, and ultimately physicians came to see them as potential threats. Although administrators did not possess medical degrees, they became forces to be reckoned with in the American Hospital Association and it became evident that their agendas were departing from those that traditionally focused on physicians. George Bugbee, assistant director of the University of Michigan's hospital in 1938, and other hospital administrators moved to develop a new American College of Hospital Administrators (later the American College of Healthcare Executives [ACHE]). Established in 1933, the founders were intent that this organization be separate from the American Hospital Association and serve the professional interests of both non-medical as well as physician administrators.

Some physician administrators saw the establishment of this organization as an attempt to take hospital administration duties away from physician managers and give them to non-physician managers. However, the new college for administrators was successful despite criticism from traditionalists, and it provided an important setting for identification and bonding for administrators. Over time physicians came to see that rather than being competitors for power, administrators provided important business and administrative functions that freed doctors to concentrate on medical issues, which, after all, were their primary concern.

Professional Organizations: A Big Umbrella

The first health care managers were hospital administrators. But as the population increased, and health institutions grew with the population, other occupations began to be defined under the umbrella of "health care administration." Group practice administrators, marketing and public relations professionals, academicians in public health or policy issues, nursing home and long-term care administrators, consultants, insurance professionals, professional and trade group executives, social workers, and others are all now considered health care administrators. A good way to see how some of these groups joined underneath the umbrella of hospital administrators is to look at the development of their professional organizations, which now exert a great deal of influence on health policy and practices.

Medical Group Practices

As early as 1926 a group of clinic managers met in Madison, Wisconsin, and formed the National Association of Clinic Managers. The name was changed to the Medical Group Management Association (MGMA) in 1963 to reflect the diverse management roles found in group practice. MGMA is the nation's principal voice for the medical group management profession. The mission of MGMA is to continually improve the performance of medical group practice professionals and the organizations they represent. MGMA serves 22,500 members who lead and manage more than 13,700 organizations in which almost 275,000 physicians practice. Its diverse membership comprises administrators, CEOs, physicians in management, board members, office managers, and many other management professionals. They work in medical practices and ambulatory care organizations of all sizes and types, including integrated systems and hospital- and medical school-affiliated practices.

Health Care Consulting

Health care institutions often hire outside consultants to advise them in areas of expertise that they do not have on-site. Recommendations in areas such as strategy, finance, marketing, governance, executive development, and more are frequently delivered by consultants. In 1949, it was recognized that a professional membership organization was needed to apply standards and credentialing for consultants so that health care institutions could rely on quality advice. The American Association of Healthcare Consultants (AAHC) was founded to provide these services and to further the education and networking opportunities for members.

Health Care Finance

The Health Care Financial Management Association (HFMA) was founded in 1946 as the American Association of Hospital Accountants, taking their current name in 1968. With over 35,000 members, it is the nation's leading membership organization for health care financial management executives and leaders. Their purpose is to define, realize, and advance the financial management of health care by helping members and others improve the business performance of organizations operating in or serving the health care field. Their members range from CFOs to controllers to accountants and members can be found in all areas of the health care system, including hospitals, managed care organizations, physician practices, accounting firms, and insurance companies.

Marketing and Public Relations

Large hospital centers and even group practices found it necessary to adopt business marketing and public relations practices in order to get the message out for their services and to bring the community into their delivery environment. With the complexities of aligning with community needs, speaking for a health institution's successes (and sometimes failures), sorting through the tangle of ever-changing legislative guidelines, and generally upholding the reputation of the institution, marketing and public relations professionals became critical to the function of these organizations. This type of health care professional is here to stay. Historically, these professionals have not been in the health care environment for very long. It appears that about 40 years ago, the movement to establish marketing and public relations departments in health facilities began to gear up as these facilities became more complex. Their professional organizations are largely regional, and they function to bring together professionals who serve in the capacity of public relations and marketing professionals in the health care industry.

The Healthcare Public Relations and Marketing Association (HPRMA) is an affiliate of the American Hospital Association. It is located in Southern California and primarily addresses the needs of marketing and public relations in that area. Similarly, the Health Care Public Relations and Marketing Society (HCPRMS) serves professionals in southeast Wisconsin. The Healthcare Public Relations and Marketing Society of Greater New York was founded in 1969 by a group of health care public relations and marketing executives. Their goal was to create a forum to foster professional growth and regular interaction among colleagues within the field.

Health Information Systems

Health care technology is more important than ever, with new advances being made in both equipment and information. The need for a specialty was realized in the late 1950s, and in 1961 the Healthcare Information Management Systems Society (HIMSS) was founded. Focused on providing global leadership for the optimal use of health care information technology (IT) and management systems for the betterment of health care, this membership organization represents more than 20,000 individual members. Additionally, there are over 350 corporate members, including many international organizations.

Human Resources

Health care organizations are governed by unique regulatory and compliance laws and issues, and there are unions that represent various segments of health care workers. In 1964, the American Society for Healthcare Human Resources Administration (ASHHRA) was founded to meet the professional needs of human resources professionals in health care who deal with these unique circumstances. With more than 3,350 members, the organization seeks to establish best practices in the delivery of human resource services in a health care setting.

Health Care Facilities: Standardization and Accreditation

Attempts had been made to standardize hospital care as far back as 1917, but things got serious in 1951 when a consortium of health organizations established the Joint Commission on Accreditation of Hospitals (JCAH)—a nonprofit organization designed to provide standards for voluntary accreditation. Over the years, the commission has developed a rigorous set of standards that are now used to evaluate the compliance of 16,000 institutions. The evaluation process helps these institutions improve their systems, which results in better patient care. For instance, critical care units of hospitals are evaluated as to whether they have the capability to sustain themselves in case of a water or fuel emergency for 96 hours. Another important initiative by the Joint Commission is to institute measurement systems that evaluate performance standards. Activities in health care institutions that do not conform to the performance standards are monitored until improvement is achieved.

Now, the accreditation process has extended beyond hospitals to long-term care facilities, psychiatric facilities, ambulatory care centers, laboratories, and other facilities. The organization changed its name to reflect its broader mission to the Joint Commission on Accreditation of Healthcare Organizations, but it is now known simply as the Joint Commission.

Educational Programs: Support and Accreditation

With the development of many educational programs in the 20th century, it became necessary—if the field was to be taken seriously and seen as a viable occupational option—to devise ways to evaluate the health care administration programs and to accredit the worthy ones. Two organizations were formed that addressed these needs.

The Association of University Programs in Health Administration (AUPHA) is a non-profit membership organization comprised of university-based educational programs, faculty, practitioners, and provider organizations. Its purpose is to serve as a kind of clearinghouse where quality programs can be supported and acknowledged in service of promoting excellence in health care management education. They do this through providing opportunities for networking and through providing tools, research, conferences, and forums.

AUPHA grew out of the efforts of the W. K. Kellogg Foundation to professionalize the management of hospitals following World War II. In 1948, the Joint Commission on Education for Hospital Administration, which was established by the foundation, presented a report that called for the expansion of university graduate programs in health care administration and provided guidelines for their content. The first formal meeting of AUPHA took place in 1949 and included these founding programs: the University of Chicago, Northwestern University, Columbia University, the University of Minnesota, the University of Toronto, Washington University, and Yale University. University undergraduate programs seeking full membership are accredited through the AUPHA, and today there are over 150 graduate and undergraduate programs in North America.

While undergraduate accreditation is available through AUPHA, graduate accreditation is available through the Commission on Accreditation of Healthcare Management Education, or the CAHME. The original accrediting mechanisms for CAHME were first established along with the creation of AUPHA in 1948. This organization sets criteria for quality graduate programs in health care management education and accredits programs that meet those criteria. CAHME performs a public service by maintaining quality in such programs and disseminating information about the appropriate programs to students and early careerists. Programs accredited by CAHME are housed in different settings within the university including schools of business, medicine, public health, public administration, allied health sciences, and graduate studies. A variety of degrees reflect the disciplinary focus of the program such as MA, MBA, MHA, MHSA, MPH, MS, and others.

CAHME has been granted formal recognition by the United States Department of Education (DOE) and Council on Higher Education Accreditation (CHEA) as the only organization to accredit master's level health care management programs in the United States and Canada. Undergraduate programs accredited by AUPHA and graduate programs accredited by CAHME are listed in the "Resources" chapter.

Where We Are Today

The field of health care administration has changed dramatically. Cynthia Haddock and her colleagues (2002) state that there are three primary objectives that concern health care administrators today. First, they are responsible for the business and financial aspects of hospitals, clinics, and other health services organization. As such, they are focused on increasing efficiency and financial stability. Their roles include human resources management, financial management, cost accounting, data collection and analysis, strategic planning, marketing, and the various maintenance functions of the organization. Second, health care administrators are responsible for providing care to dependent people at the most vulnerable times of their lives. Third, administrators are responsible for maintaining the moral and social order of their organizations, serving as advocates for patients, arbitrators in situations where there are competing values, and intermediaries for the various professional groups that practice within the organization.

INTERVIEW

Mission to the World

Dr. Oscar Aylor
Director of Mercy Ministries, Mission to the World, Atlanta, Georgia

How did you get into the health care administration industry?
I got into it like a lot of people did by starting out with an interest in medicine. While I was at the University of Virginia, I wanted to be a doctor one year and the next year I did not. I did not have a long-term focus, even though I was intrigued by medicine because I had a grandfather who was a country doctor and I used to follow him around on his house calls. Just as I was graduating, a fraternity brother who had the same interests asked me if I had ever heard of hospital administration. I looked into it and it appealed to me, so I applied to a few graduate programs right out of college. I did not get accepted because they said I needed some experience first and to come back later. So, I got some experience at my hometown hospital doing a variety of things from helping the credit manager and personnel director to doing EKGs. I went to graduate school later when I was 27 for an MSHA (Master of Science in Hospital Administration).

What do you think are some of the issues in the field now?
We have a lot of problems. One is that we have to get better care to the growing immigrant population. Another is that too many people are experiencing a loss of insurance coverage. Also, there are too many people that experience access problems to existing health care resources. There are frustrating issues of cost and quality. When these things happen, it does not just affect the individuals, it affects the whole community.

What are some of the highlights of the history of the field, and what trends emerged as a result of it?
The modern hospital began in the late 1800s. Harvard (1870) and then Johns Hopkins (1890) began introducing science into the curriculum, had research programs, and established medical schools and residency programs. Physicians were resistant to science in those days. That is, they believed that patient care and science were not connected in important enough ways to affect their relationships with patients. That all changed with the Flexner Report, which was issued in 1910.

Abraham Flexner was commissioned by the Carnegie Foundation to evaluate the quality of medical education. Flexner made appointments with medical school deans, who thought he was going to award them funds from the foundation. But what he did was find that only about 75 percent of the medical schools existing then needed to survive, and the rest really could not justify their existence. That report put a lot of medical schools out of business and consolidated others. The number of schools quickly went from 131 to 95 within a few years.

After that, medical education along with hospitals became more sophisticated and complex. Doctors did not have time to run them. They were much more interested in doing surgery, using the new technology, and making money. It was about that time that the health care administration field began to thrive because of the need for business rigor in the hospitals.

How would you characterize the relationship between medical professionals and health care administrators?
This varies from institution to institution. If an administrator is skilled at coordinating efforts to bring these groups together, it is reflected in the success of the institution. The turnover rate of administrators tells the story. If there is too much turnover, then the relationships have not been worked out adequately. It requires better than sufficient interpersonal skills on the part of the administrator. There is still a strain in some quarters. But with the younger generation coming along, relationships between clinical staff and administrators are getting better. Both sides are beginning to think more alike. Technology has bridged a lot of that. With both working on EMR [electronic medical records], patient safety issues, and other technological issues, we are more comfortable sitting at the same table than we used to be.

What are the trends in public health that have affected administrators?
[One] trend that occurred that was important to the profession is when the interests of hospitals and those of public health diverged around 1915. Hospitals became more interested in treatment and surgery, and public health professionals pushed prevention. Those two streams were on separate paths, and they were uncomfortable with one another. Physicians, for instance, who went into public health were marginalized. Administrators who worked for health departments were treated the same way. What began to change this were the events of 9/11/2001[the attacks on the World Trade Center in New

(continues on next page)

INTERVIEW

Mission to the World (continued)

York]. With my peers, it was like the light was turned on. We realized that we all live in a world of public health. We have to be concerned about security, safety, population health. The streams started to converge at that moment. We are all much more concerned with public health than we used to be, and we are all more comfortable with the idea of prevention.

What do you think will happen to health care now?
Not all the big, famous medical institutions in the United States can survive over the long haul. There is not enough money to reimburse overhead for all the beds that exist. Also, there will be a continuing emphasis on prevention, on more outpatient care, and on shorter inpatient stays. Some say the hospital of the future will consist of an ICU [intensive care unit] and an emergency room.

If I were looking into the future, I would think we would have to emphasize prevention and legitimate research. The focus on inpatient care is on the way out. We need to provide more and better care on an outpatient basis. We need to plan better, especially on a system wide basis. We need to look at the health care needs of the United States and compare them to what is happening in areas outside our country, continuing to look for best practices. We need to find ways to coordinate the delivery of health services to a greater extent within our own institutions.

From a rocky start, health care management has evolved into a major business in the 21st century, run like any other business with many of the same concerns. A major difference, of course, is that those involved in this business have the end user's—the patient—well-being as a primary focus. Although it appears that many of the early conflicts and challenges have been worked through—establishment of roles, conflict with physicians, creating funding mechanisms for their institutions—new challenges arise every day. Today members of the health care management field—at about 262,000 individuals—comprise a critical mass with which to confront these challenges. Moreover, the over 30 professional organizations that represent these individuals do important advocacy work that leads to major changes in the health care system.

Some who have been professionals in health care for some time believe that the field has gotten too large and there are too many separate groups within it, each with its own agenda. Others say it is still a "hidden" career in some respects because many are puzzled about the roles and requirements of health care administrators. Nonetheless, after a little more than a hundred years of recent history the industry is well-established and geared to expand.

A Brief Chronology

1728-1686 B.C.E.: Hammurabi, a Babylonian king, creates the first code of written laws which includes the first record of regulation of doctor's practices.

480 B.C.E.: Hippocrates comes up with a rational approach to medicine, developing surgical procedures and providing records of surgeries. He wrote the Hippocratic Oath that defines to this day the scientific and ethical obligations of physicians.

369 C.E.: The first Christian hospital is built by Justinian and Fabiola in Rome.

7th Century: A system of Islamic hospitals is established—especially in Baghdad, Damascus, and Cairo—that included insane asylums a full ten centuries before they first appeared in Europe.

Middle Ages: Religious communities assume responsibility for the sick and build hospitals throughout Europe, but they were the last resort for the sick and dying.

15th, 16th, and 17th Centuries In the New World: Hospitals are built by religious orders and by explorers in Santo Domingo, Mexico, Quebec, and Montreal. In New Amsterdam (now New York), an alms house is built in 1658 that eventually grew into Bellevue Hospital.

1751: The Pennsylvania Hospital is founded by Benjamin Franklin and Thomas Bond to provide a place for Philadelphia physicians to hospitalize their private patients.

1771: New York Hospital is established as a private hospital and paid for by contributions from farmers and merchants.

1798: The United States Marine Hospital Service Act mandates hospital care for disabled seamen and opens the way for the first Marine Hospital built in Norfolk, Virginia, in 1802.

Fast Facts

The Medical Trade

Until Johns Hopkins Medical School opened in 1893, most medical students were taught in "trade schools" which, because they were set up to turn a profit, often accepted high school graduates who would have had trouble getting into a liberal arts college. After two, at most three, years of attending typically repetitious lectures by part-time teachers, students were free to apprentice themselves to older doctors or simply hang out a shingle, even if they had never laid a hand on a patient.

1853: The New York Infirmary for Women and Children is opened by Elizabeth Blackwell, the first woman to earn a medical degree in the United States.

1887: Founding of the National Institutes of Health.

1890s: The Association of Hospital Superintendents is created, which later becomes the American Hospital Association (AHA).

End of 19th Century: There are 149 hospitals in the United States with 35,500 beds.

1900: The first educational program for nurse administrators is established at Columbia Teacher's College in New York.

1917: *Minimum Standards for Hospitals*, a document, is adopted by the American College of Surgeons.

1926: The National Association of Clinic Managers is founded. It later was named the Medical Group Management Association (MGMA).

1928: The first hospital administration program graduates two women from Marquette University.

1933: The American College of Hospital Administrators is formed, which later becomes the American College of Healthcare Executives (ACHE).

1930s: The National Hospital Association, an organization for African-American health care administrators, is established.

1934: The first graduate program in health care administration is established at the University of Chicago.

1935: National Labor Relations Act provides for collective bargaining in hospitals and health services organizations.

1946: The American Association of Hospital Accountants is established and is later named Healthcare Financial Management Association (HFMA). The Hill-Burton Act mandates four billion dollars of federal money for the building and improvement of hospitals.

1948: The Association of University Programs in Health Administration (AUPHA) is created to promote excellence in undergraduate and graduate programs in health care administration.

1951: The Joint Commission of the Accreditation of Hospitals (JCAH) is formed and later becomes the premiere accreditation body for health care facilities in the United States.

1960: Federal programs are instituted to train more physicians.

1966: The Medicare and Medicaid Bills are passed by Congress.

1968: The Accrediting Commission on Graduate Education for Health Administration is formed to accredit graduate programs. It is now named CAHME (Commission on Accreditation of Healthcare Management Education).

1970: The Occupational Safety and Health Act (OSHA) was passed. It requires employers to maintain a safe working environment for health care employees.

1982: Tax Equity and Fiscal Responsibility Act (TEFRA) passed to control Medicare costs.

Beginning of 21st Century: According to the Bureau of Labor Statistics, 96,910 health care managers are employed by hospitals, 23,610 by physician offices, 17,960 in nursing care facilities, 13,810 in home health care, and 12,030 in outpatient care centers.

2003: The Health Insurance and Portability and Accountability Act (HIPAA) was passed. It protects employees from outside access to personal health information and limits employers' ability to use employee health information under health insurance plans.

Chapter 2

State of the Industry

Every industry has a set of indicators that define its current state and its relative health compared to other industries. They build identities through what is known about the industry's performance in the marketplace and the activities that consolidate its mission and function. Health care management is no exception. Statistics on numbers employed, wages, trends—current and future—important technology, conferences and industry events, industry forces, and issues of law and government all make up the personality of an industry. With the help of some information from the Bureau of Labor Statistics, let us look at basic facts and then at a discussion of prospects, the future job outlook, and earnings.

Employment

Several indicators demonstrate that the field is expanding and will continue to do so. The Bureau of Labor Statistics states that medical and health services managers held about 262,000 jobs in 2006. About 35 percent worked in hospitals, and another 22 percent worked in offices of physicians or in nursing and residential care facilities. Most of the remainder worked in home health care services, federal government health care facilities, outpatient care centers, insurance carriers, and community care facilities for the elderly. Health care settings range from small-town private physician practices who employ one medical assistant to large inner-city hospitals that provide thousands of diverse jobs. In 2006, almost half of non-hospital health care establishments employed fewer than five workers. By contrast, seven out of 10 hospital workers were in establishments with more than 1,000 workers.

Job Outlook

From 2006 to 2016, the employment of health care managers is expected to grow 16 percent—faster than average for all occupations—bringing the number of health services managers up to 305,000. This field is expanding because the need for health care services parallels both the growth and the aging of the population. As the need for doctors, nurses, respiratory technicians, X-ray technologists, IT professionals, and those in other health-related occupations grows, the need increases for more facilities and for more trained managers to run them.

Of course, a big imponderable is the effect of the Patient Protection and Affordable Care Act on the American health care system. This new plan will add many more people to be served by the health system. The proponents of the public option part of the health care bills in Congress point to the fact that 47 to 50 million people will enter the health care system as current or future patients. Managers in all settings will be needed to improve quality and efficiency of health care at the same time that they control costs, as insurance companies and Medicare demand higher levels of accountability. Managers also will be needed to oversee the computerization of patient records and to ensure their security as required by law. Additional demand for managers will stem from the need to recruit workers and increase employee retention, to comply with changing regulations, to implement new technology, and to help improve the health of their communities by emphasizing preventive care.

Hospitals will continue to employ the most medical and health services managers over the 2006–16 decade. However, the number of new jobs created is expected to increase at a slower rate in hospitals than in many other industries because of the growing use of clinics and other outpatient care sites. Employment will grow fastest in practitioners' offices and in home health care agencies. Many services previously provided in hospitals will continue to shift to these settings, especially as medical technologies improve. Demand in medical group practice management will grow as medical group practices become larger and more complex.

Medical and health services managers also will be employed by health care management companies that provide management services to hospitals and other organizations and to specific departments such as emergency, information management systems, managed care contract negotiations, and physician recruiting.

Job Prospects

Job opportunities will be good, and applicants with work experience in the health care field and strong business management skills should have the best opportunities. Medical and health services managers with experience in large hospital facilities will enjoy an advantage in the job market, as hospitals become larger and more complex. According to the American Hospital Association, absolute numbers of hospitals are not predicted to increase significantly but the trend toward hospital systems that include laboratories, group practices, ambulatory care facilities, and ancillary care will increase. Competition for jobs at the highest management levels will be keen because of the high pay and prestige.

Earnings

Median annual earnings for medical and health services managers were $73,340 in May 2006. This median includes everyone from an entry-level finance employee to the COO of a hospital. The middle 50 percent earned between $57,240 and $94,780. The lowest 10 percent earned less than $45,050, and the highest 10 percent earned more than $127,830. Median annual earnings in the industries employing the largest numbers of medical and health services managers in May 2006 include the following salaries:

General medical and surgical hospitals	$78,660
Outpatient care centers	$69,920
Offices of physicians	$67,540
Nursing care facilities	$66,730
Home health care services	$66,720

Senior-level positions in health care management can be quite competitive. A recent survey reported by Hewitt Associates, a consulting and management search firm, shows the following median

Fast Facts

Business Versus Practice

Cynthia Robinson, a health care practice consultant at Davenport, Marvin, Joyce & Co., LLP–an accounting, consulting, and wealth management firm in Greensboro, North Carolina–reports that the business side of health care has become more important in practices and will continue to do so. In fact, in some practices physicians feel that the business side is taking far too much time away from their practices. They often declare that they want to treat patients and have someone else handle administration.

compensations (including fringe benefits and bonuses) for health care executives:

President/CEO	$270,000
Associate Administrator/COO	$210,800
Chief Financial Officer/CFO	$153,480
Director of Information Systems/CIO	$102,600
Director of Human Resources	$99,700

Earnings in the West were highest, and earnings the Southeast were the lowest among regions.

In another survey sponsored by the American College of Health-care Executives (ACHE), several recent recipients of master's degrees in health care administration were interviewed. Entry-level managers were compensated at a median of $49,684, middle managers at $60,794, and executives at $99,620.

Earnings of medical and health services managers vary by type and size of the facility and by level of responsibility. For example, the Medical Group Management Association reported that, in 2006, median salaries for administrators were $72,875 in practices with six or fewer physicians, $95,766 in practices with seven to 25 physicians, and $132,955 in practices with 26 or more physicians.

According to a 2006 survey by the Professional Association of Health Care Office Management, the average total compensation for office managers in specialty physicians' practices was $70,474 in gastroenterology, $70,599 in dermatology, $76,392 in cardiology, $67,317 in ophthalmology, $67,222 in obstetrics and gynecology, $77,621 in orthopedics, $62,125 in pediatrics, $66,853 in internal medicine, and $60,040 in family practice.

Major Issues and Trends

Things happen, especially in a $2.5-trillion industry like health care in the United States. Whenever major events occur at any level in the health care industry, it affects administrators who as the implementers are in the front line. Beaufort Longest and Kurt Darr (2008), academicians with expertise in health management and policy issues, provide some invaluable insights with respect to these central trends.

Controlling Costs

State and federal governments have been scrambling to control the costs of their health services programs. This trend will continue, and will focus on hospitals, which consume about one-third of health expenditures. Economic pressures will be exerted to discharge patients quickly, maybe even more quickly than sound practice warrants. Hospitals will take care of the most acute cases, because those who are less sick tend to be treated in alternative environments. This results in greater financial pressure in hospitals, because care of the acutely ill costs more, potentially meaning that the costs per hospitalization will rise.

Competition

The competitive environment that emerged in the late 1970s and early 1980s has continued. Inefficient institutions do not survive in this environment, or if they do they are providing substandard care. Hospitals and hospital systems are subject to bankruptcies, mergers, and joint activities. Increasingly, hospitals will be connected to one another through shared services, group purchasing, and strategic alliances. However, health systems will remain local and regional rather than national under such a system.

Focus on the Patient

In the 1980s, there was a spate of corporate restructuring undertaken by hospitals driven by a concern for cost containment. New
payment systems were introduced, staffs were downsized, lengths
of stay were shortened, and many more changes were initiated as
hospitals focused on business issues to the detriment of the patient.
Although largely well intended, these initiatives resulted in turmoil
in many hospitals and were ultimately deemed unsuccessful, even
though they protected hospitals' assets and expanded their range
of activities. The effort resulted in management's losing sight of the
core business—serving the patient. By the mid-1990s, hospitals had
divested themselves of non-core businesses and focused their full
attention to their original reasons for being—the patients.

Physicians and Health Services Organizations

Tim Rice, CEO of a major hospital system, asserts that one of the major
trends for hospital systems today is that they employ more and more
physicians. Many more practices are becoming part of integrated health
systems that include multispecialty hospitals, group practices, laboratories, and ambulatory care facilities. This trend is growing because it
reduces costs and increases efficiency. Such systems contain a variety
of group practices with special compensation structures developed for
physicians. These structures serve as incentives for doctors, and the
configuration of the group practices has many advantages for them in
terms of purchasing, negotiating contracts, and so forth. The system
also works for the hospital, because the physicians have departmental responsibilities within the institution, such as serving as staff in
clinical departments. The hospital also benefits from having patients
referred to them from the group practices.

Management Challenges

Health care managers work in an increasingly complex and diverse
society, and the following trends that have emerged over the years
have reflected this.

Diversity
The U.S. Census Bureau projects that by 2050, nearly 50 percent of
the overall U.S. population will be composed of minority groups.

Health care managers who supervise people of other cultures and ethnicities have to adapt to the "new normal" and not necessarily hold on to standards that apply to homogeneous groups. Leadership styles and management strategies need to be evaluated for their effectiveness in addressing diversity in employee and client populations.

Knowledge

People who know how things work and share this information with others are increasingly driving organizations. There is pressure to apply new knowledge to challenges as they arise. The health care manager needs to know how to manage knowledge workers, such as information technology experts, and how to optimize the knowledge environment by creating systems wherein ideas can be shared and ultimately brought into practice.

Teamwork

Health care organizations are increasingly driven by teams that put together individuals with different skills in order to create a high-functioning unit. Treatment teams, for example, might consist of a physician, nurses, a social worker, a therapist, an officer, and specialized medical assistants.

Empowerment

Upper management does not do all the decision-making in the modern workplace. Health care managers at every level will be called upon to work things out on their own and provide solutions to thorny problems.

National Health Insurance

I suffer no illusions that this will be an easy process. It will be hard. But I also know that nearly a century after Teddy Roosevelt first called for reform, the cost of our health care has weighed down our economy and the conscience of our nation long enough. So let there be no doubt: health care reform cannot wait, it must not wait, and it will not wait another year.

—President Barack Obama, February 24, 2009

There it is—right from the top. According to the White House Web site, $7,421 was spent by the United States on every American for health care in 2007. That is more than twice the amount spent by all other developed nations and more than is spent on food or housing. If this continues, by 2050 one out of very four dollars in our economy will be spent on health care. This, of course, is unsustainable because it affects the economy and inhibits growth in other sectors.

Even with the recent passage of health care reform by the U.S. House and Senate, health care managers still have an active role in shaping the issue. The policy statements from the professional organizations reflect various levels of support for reform. The American College of Healthcare Executives (ACHE) supports providing coverage for the uninsured. The Medical Group Management Association (MGMA) has written a letter to the congressional committee asking for provisions on medical liability. There is a wait-and-see environment for health care managers as the coming changes are gradually being implemented.

Technology

Any discussion about the technology involved in health care is a long one. Medical equipment is being developed so rapidly that it is hard to keep up with it—robotic technologies, drug advancements, 64-slice CT scanners, Picture Archive Communication Systems (PACs) that reduce the need for storage for X-ray films, just to name a very few. All of these innovations affect needs for staff and change service structures, which ultimately impact the job of the health care administrators. By examining just one aspect of technological developments—information technology—you can get a glimpse of the ubiquitous, pervasive, and continually changing technological environment under which health care managers must work.

Electronic Medical Records (EMR)—Coming to a doctor's office or hospital near you

Technology is a great tool in documenting medical information, and various forms are used by health care administrators, physicians, patients, support services, business office staff, pharmacists, therapists, dentists, mental health providers, imaging providers, accrediting bodies, government workers, and insurers. Carla Wiggins, a professor of health care administration, states in *Introduction to Health Care Management* by Sharon B. Buchinder and Nancy H. Shanks that health care is information intense. Every interaction must be documented, and if it is not, then the interaction is considered not to have occurred. Lack of documentation raises havoc with the accreditation bodies like the Joint Commission on Accreditation of Healthcare Organizations (JCAHO), who assess quality assurance by examining quality of documentation. If a hospital is not accredited, it cannot receive Medicare or Medicaid payments.

Unfortunately, despite new technologies, medical information is still usually in the form of a paper chart that may be incomplete, bloated, and full of illegible writing. The great revolution in health care informatics is the electronic medical record (EMR). Systems are becoming available, but many physician's offices, hospitals, and other health care facilities are at different stages of adopting them. This makes for a confused landscape wherein one or two hospitals in a city may have their records entirely computerized, and the rest are either in the process or have not yet started. So, the passage of information still has to be done the old way—by transmission of parts of a paper chart. In addition, some physicians are not quite there yet with the concept of EMR. Cynthia Robinson explains that EMR can frustrate some doctors who believe that the pointing and clicking involved takes away from patient interaction. They put it off, get frustrated with technology, and ultimately get behind on their input.

What does an ideal EMR system look like? In its best form, EMR can provide caregivers with immediate access to decision support, expert knowledge, care prompts, reminders, alerts, and connectivity to the Internet, e-mail, and other tools. It can also automatically record billing charges and enter the use of materials into the organization's inventory control system. EMR will dramatically change the way that health organizations do business, and administrators—not just IT specialists—will play a major role in implementing these systems and fostering their success.

On the Cutting Edge

EMR

Electronic medical records (EMR) are a great tool for physicians to get on-the-spot comparative information on a diagnosis. For example, a physician who would like to discuss a patient's diagnosis could click on a link and obtain data on how common the diagnosis is, discover the most common treatment within the region or the nation, and find the most recent research on the patient's diagnosis, treatment, and outcome probabilities.

More Informatics

There are other technologies being used in health care settings, or are being considered, that are enhancing quality and efficiency. *Computerized physician order entry (CPOE)* is a handheld device that records and reports a physician's orders, which helps diminish the number of medication errors (98,000 patients die each year from this cause) and also includes information about side effects and dosage issues. *Bar coding* that is encrypted with patient-specific information is used on patient wrist bands and is scanned whenever medication is ordered. *Telehealth* is an electronic system that facilitates the delivery of health information and health care to people in distant locations. It provides educational services, access to digital health information when available, interactive conferencing, consultation, and health exams. *Enterprise resource planning (ERP)* is an overarching system that allows interoperability among all the computers and information systems in an organization. This would mean that information would only have to be entered once before being accessed by different users, who, for instance, would be able to schedule appointments online. Additionally, physicians would have access to all patient information. This is still in the dreaming stage for most health care organizations.

Key Players

If you ask many health care administrators, they will probably tell you that they see, hear, and experience the effects of two major influences in their daily work: the government and the industry's professional and trade organizations.

The Government: Wherever You Look

Paul Feldstein, a professor of economics and health care management, says that government has a significant role in health care in two major ways: first, in financing, and second, in regulation. On the financing end, hospital and physician services are financed for the aged (Medicare), for the poor (Medicaid), and for active military and veterans.

There is also a large network of state and county hospitals subsidized by the government. Health professional schools are subsidized, and loan programs for students in the health professions are guaranteed by the government. Employer-paid health insurance is excluded from taxable income. These programs and others make government a 45 percent partner in total health expenditures.

Regulation

Then there is regulation. State licensing boards determine the criteria for entry into the health professions. Practice regulations determine which tasks can be performed by which professional groups. In some states hospital investment is subject to state review. Prices for services under Medicare are regulated, and health insurance companies are regulated by the states. There are numerous labor laws to ensure workplace equity and protect employees in varying circumstances that apply to health care organizations and that are enforced by the federal and state governments. Some recent notable legislative initiatives that apply to health care are the anti-kickback statute that disallows laboratories and other services kicking back Medicare payments to physicians, the Stark law that prohibits a physician's referral of Medicare patients to an entity for the furnishing of health services (if there is a financial relationship between the physician and the entity), and several antitrust laws directed at mergers of providers that suppress competition.

Health care managers at the most general level need to be aware of the financial and regulatory environment. Depending on their specialty, a deeper knowledge may be required. For example, a human resources professional working in a hospital would have to be aware of the labor laws that govern hiring and working practices in the state. Also, knowledge of union rules is necessary because some groups like nurses, housekeeping staff, and facilities managers may be members. Practice managers, as well as hospital finance administrators, will be subject to the rules governing Medicare and Medicaid. This is a big responsibility that some administrators find quite onerous.

The Health Insurance Portability and Accountability Act (HIPAA)

Administrators will run into HIPAA in all health care industry settings. Passed by Congress in 1996, the Centers for Medicare & Medicaid Services Web site (http://www.cms.gov) reports that HIPAA establishes national standards for electronic health care transactions and national identifiers for providers, health plans, and employers. It also addressed the security and privacy of health data. In other words, HIPAA sets the rules to be followed by doctors, hospitals, and other health care providers that help ensure that all medical records, medical billing, and patient accounts meet certain consistent standards. In addition, HIPAA requires that all patients be able access their own medical records, correct any errors or omissions, and be informed about how personal information is used. In many cases, HIPAA provisions have led to extensive overhauling of medical records and billing systems.

Professional Organizations: The Influencers

Because the scope of health care management covers a wide area of professions and competencies, organizations have been created to serve the needs of individuals in just about every part of the field you can name. The IT people have their own group, the marketing people have theirs, the practice administrators who have different needs than the hospital administrators have theirs, and so on. These groups have acted as major drivers in shaping the jobs of health care administrators in their specialties, and they are also important in their roles as influencers of policy and government regulation.

Below are some of the better-known organizations that wield a major influence in the health care administration world. The listings include information about these organizations' major conferences, educational programs, credentialing guidelines and offerings, career services, and, importantly, their roles as advocates for issues that affect health administrators.

American Academy of Medical Administrators (AAMA)

AAMA is an association of multidisciplinary health care managers at all levels and within any kind of health care setting. Its 2,500 members have access to specialty colleges like those for specialists in contingency planning, oncology, rural health care, and federal health care that provide educational and networking opportunities.

Conferences: An annual conference is held that focuses on keynote speakers, over 30 concurrent sessions, exhibitors that bring the latest in professional products and services, and networking opportunities. Sessions are presented in such areas as cardiovascular administration, contingency planning, health care information administration, health plan management, oncology administration, federal health care administration, and health care leadership. In addition to the annual conference, other conferences are held throughout the year on specific subjects.

Education: AAMA maintains an extensive educational program called EduLink that offers over 2,000 online programs plus frequent Webinars. Examples of the titles of courses being offered are

"Managing Information Overload," "Business Ethics for Managers," and "American Disabilities Act." There are over 488 courses offered in office software and many more in the categories of preparing for change and management fundamentals.

Credentialing: AAMA offers two types of credentials in general health care administration and in various specialties of this multifaceted profession:

- Examination-based credentials (CAAMA; Credential Member of the American Academy of Medical Adminis-trators) are earned by passing an examination based on a specified Body of Knowledge in health care administra-tion, as defined by AAMA.

- Experience-based credentials (FAAMA, Fellow of AAMA; Diplomate; FACCA, Fellow the American Academy of Contingency Planners; and FACCP, Fellow of the Ameri-can College of Cardiovascular Administrators) are earned by demonstration of professional development, service, and experience in health care administration through *one* of the following paths:
  - Original fellowship thesis of graduate school quality
  - Three case studies
  - Documentation of formal education, continuing education, and organizational and professional service

Career Services: There is a public job board called JobLink for both employers and for prospective job seekers. It does not appear that there are formal mentoring or career programs other than the net-working opportunities afforded by the frequent conferences.

American College of Heathcare Executives (ACHE)
ACHE is an international professional society of health care execu-tives with 37,500 members who lead hospitals, health care systems, and other health organizations.

Conferences: ACHE holds an annual Congress on Health Care Leader-ship that presents the best in professional development, opportunities to network with and learn from peers, and the latest information for career enhancement and for addressing organizational challenges in innovative ways. There are also a series of seminars on subjects concerning health care leadership and management given every month by local chapters.

Education: ACHE sponsors many educational events through their regional chapters throughout the country. For instance, in August 2009, the New York cluster offered programs in "Leadership Persuasion Skills," "Strategic Planning," and "Moving Beyond Financial Survival," among several others. There are also special programs targeted to senior executives, CEOs, ACHE fellows, and COOs at various times throughout the year. Members can access educational options through Webinars and online seminars.

Credentialing: The premier credential in health care management is becoming board certified in health care management as an ACHE Fellow (FACHE). This requires passing a Board of Governors exam as well as fulfilling several other criteria. There are also certifications given for participating in ACHE and other organizations' educational programs.

Career Services: These services are extensive for members and include a job bank, mentoring and coaching opportunities, career guides and other publications, an "Ask the Expert" online facility, resources for students and early careerists, career-focused blogs, and several other ways to access career information and options for networking.

Advocacy: ACHE publishes policy statements through their magazines and other venues in order for chapter members to use this information to influence local and federal governments. ACHE can be quite influential in government circles, since their membership comprises the most senior-level executives in the industry.

American Health Information Management Association (AHIMA)

AHIMA is the premier association of health information management (HIM) professionals. AHIMA's 53,000 members are dedicated to the effective management of personal health information required to deliver quality health care to the public. HIM encompasses a wide range of job functions, including medical records management, privacy officer, risk management, medical coding, corporate compliance, and data analysis and reporting.

Conferences: There is a yearly convention and regional meetings throughout the year. Both cover topics of interest in data management and provide networking opportunities.

Education: AHIMA offers an extensive program of audio seminars and Webinars on such subjects as medical coding and reimbursements, electronic health records (EHR), career management, health information management operations, and clinical terminology. AHIMA has its own press that publishes books of articles on the latest in health informatics.

Credentialing: Fellowship designation—FAHIMA—is available for members who have made significant contributions to the profession. AHIMA also supports a credentialing organization, the Commission on Accreditation for Health Informatics and Information Management Education (CAHIIM). CAHIIM accredits degree-granting programs in Health Informatics and Information Management that have undergone a rigorous process of voluntary peer review and have met or exceeded the minimum accreditation.

Career Services: The Web site has something called *Careerassist* where members can post résumés, network with others, and receive mentoring and coaching help.

Advocacy: AHIMA maintains an Advocacy and Public Policy Center through which they publish position papers on subjects such as the stewardship of quality health data and information. They are a source of policy information for members and encourage political action on a variety of data-related subjects. As of this writing, their policy center was actively monitoring the American Recovery Reinvestment Act (passed in February, 2009) and its impact on the industry.

American Hospital Association (AHA)

AHA is the national organization that represents and serves all types of hospitals, health care networks, and their patients and communities. Close to 5,000 hospitals, health care systems, networks, other providers of care, and 37,000 individual members come together to form the AHA. In addition to clinical members, many members are from the various areas of the health care administration field. AHA is mostly involved in representation and advocacy activities, ensuring that members' perspectives and needs are heard and addressed in national health policy development, legislative and regulatory debates, and judicial matters. Every state has at least one affiliate organization associated with the AHA, and the state organizations run the local conferences and provide educational activities.

Advocacy: Of all the organizations listed here, AHA is probably the most heavily involved in this arena. They produce many issue papers, which can be found on their Web site, and they take a strong role in advocating for their position through lobbying congressmen, issuing letters, and encouraging their members to contact their representatives. AHA is listened to by government officials because of the strength of the organization and who they represent—hospitals employ more than five million people. AHA has developed sophisticated methods of insinuating their agendas into legislative debates. Hospitals are under fire, given the ferment going on around reforming health care, and AHA is at the head of the pack in resisting some of the recommendations proposed. For instance, Medicare and Medicaid represent 55 percent of care provided by hospitals, but both programs already fall short of hospital costs of caring for patients. AHA maintains that further cuts to these programs will add to hospitals' costs deficits. In 2006, hospitals provided care at no cost to people in need at a cost of over $31 billion.

American Organization of Nurse Executives (AONE)

AONE is the national organization of nurses who design, facilitate, and manage care. The organization provides leadership, professional development, advocacy, and research in order to advance nursing practice and patient care, promote nursing leadership excellence, and shape public policy for health care.

Conferences: The annual meeting covers issues such as contemporary trends in health care that impact the nursing community, innovative delivery practices, trends in health care technology and nursing research, and networking, and includes small-group sessions in many other areas of nursing leadership.

Education: AONE sponsors a Nurse Leaders Development Track in which three-to-five day programs are given such as the Aspiring Nurse Leadership Institute, Nurse Manager Institute, and Health Policy Institute. E-programs (courseware that is available online for purchase) are also available, and individual chapters run their own programs throughout the year. A 12-month fellowship program is conducted in experiential and classroom learning for the experienced nurse manager.

Credentialing: Eligible candidates can receive the designations of Certified in Executive Nursing Practice (CENP) and Certified Nurse Manager and Leader (CNML) through taking an examination.

Career Services: AONE runs a job bank specific for nurse manager positions, has a list of executive recruiters, provides leadership and coaching resources, and compiles a library of resources relevant for the nurse manager.

Advocacy: AONE sponsors a political action group (PAC) that lobbies Capitol Hill, and it is one of the three major nursing PACs. They lobby on issues such as increasing funds for nursing education, changes to health policy, supporting research in nursing health care management, and many others.

American Public Health Association (APHA)

APHA is the oldest, largest, and most diverse organization of public health professionals in the world and has been working to improve public health since 1872. It aims to protect all Americans and their communities from preventable and serious health threats. It also strives to assure community-based health promotion and disease prevention activities and preventive health services are universally accessible in the United States. APHA represents a broad array of health professionals, with over 30,000 members in 77 disciplines and over 20,000 affiliate members.

Conferences: The annual meeting in 2009, with over 13,000 attendees, features over 1,000 scientific sessions and over 700 exhibit booths of products and services. A focus of the 2009 meeting is the 21st century challenge of water and its effects on public health. *Learning Institutes*, small focus groups that meet throughout the conference, feature such issues as assessment and planning tools for building effective public health systems, achieving evidence-based health policy, smoking cessation, and reduction in teen pregnancy.

Education: Educational offerings from APHA are limited to the scientific sessions at the annual meetings with potential to extend beyond that. The Web site, however, does have many helpful links to educational and informational resources that are relevant to public health issues.

Credentialing: APHA offers continuing education (CE) credits obtained at the Learning Institutes at the annual meeting. These are granted through other credentialing agencies that represent various aspects of health education.

Career Services: There is an online career mart that posts available jobs and where one can create and post a profile. Some jobs recently listed include health research analyst at an aircraft company, community health educator for a city agency, and occupational researcher for a private organization. The National Mentoring Program (NMP) puts together more experienced professionals with early and mid-careerists in order to increase the professional success and productivity of public health students and professionals, maximize their training, and help strengthen the field of public health through the retention and growth of committed members.

Advocacy: APHA wields a lot of clout through their extensive advocacy work. The organization works with key decision-makers to shape public policy to address today's ongoing public health concerns including ensuring access to care, protecting funding for core public health programs and services, and eliminating health disparities. They prod their members to be proactive in pushing legislation according to a health policy agenda that is disseminated to members by urging support of specific legislative actions like the Family Smoking Prevention and Tobacco Control Act, and by providing tips for approaching legislators and pushing agendas. Indeed, this group carries a very big stick in Washington and has been successful in pushing their legislative agenda in the past.

American Society for Healthcare Human Resources Administration (ASHHRA)
ASHHRA, with 3,500 members, is the only organization dedicated to meeting the professional needs of human resources professionals in the health care field.

Conferences: The annual conferences features learning sessions about acquiring techniques to help medical staff avoid burnout, retirement considerations, empowering the new generation of employees, and more. The conference also includes expert panels, special interest sessions, and networking opportunities.

Education: The organization provides frequent Webinars on relevant topics and is currently forming a Leadership Institute.

Career Services: ASHHRA runs a mentoring program that puts together an experienced person with someone who wants assistance on critical issues. On their Web site, they provide what they call *best practices*, including links to several articles and other sources—some of which offer career advice.

Advocacy: Positions on legislative issues are published on their Web site, and they encourage members to contact legislators to support those positions. For instance, they advocated for *The Secret Ballot Protection Act* that allows union members a secret vote in union organizing elections and wrote official letters of support to the bill's authors—Representatives John Kline, Jim DeMint, and Howard McKeon.

Association of Health Care Administrative Professionals (AHCAP)

AHCAP is a professional development and recognition society for executive assistants and administrative professionals in health care. With over 600 members, it is the largest society dedicated to health care executive assistants.

Conferences: The annual conference features keynote speakers, concurrent sessions, and general sessions along with sessions that give tips for maintaining personal balance, health, and an optimistic outlook in the busy medical environment. General sessions deal with such issues as knowledge sharing, leadership, enhancing skill sets, and more.

Education: Webinars on a variety of helpful subjects relevant to medical office management are offered frequently. The organization's Web site also provides information on other educational opportunities available from related organizations.

Credentialing: The certified health care administrative professional designation (cHAP) is awarded to those who have amassed and demonstrated the highest and most comprehensive levels of experience, training, and continuing education in the field of health care administration.

Career Services: There is no formal program, but the Web site lists links to a variety of career resources like educational development organizations and writers' workshops. Employers are encouraged to advertise on the site, but there is no job bank.

Advocacy: There are no formal activities in this area. This group seemingly aligns itself with other groups, like the American Hospital Association, when lobbying efforts are considered.

Healthcare Financial Management Association (HFMA)

HFMA is the nation's leading membership organization for health care financial management executives and leaders. More than 35,000 members—ranging from CFOs to controllers to accountants—consider HFMA a respected thought leader on top trends and issues facing the health care industry. HFMA members can be found in all areas of the health care system, including hospitals, managed care organizations, physician practices, accounting firms, and insurance companies.

Conferences: The national conference features keynote speakers—in June of 2009, Al Gore spoke on "Thinking Green"—and daily sessions that focus on compliance issues, antitrust regulations, taxation, investment strategies, cost savings, and other financial issues that affect health care management in their own particular ways. Interactive sessions and peer-to-peer case studies provide a forum for participants to share their experiences and learn from others.

Education: Throughout the year, there are several education options available including audio webcasts, seminars, workshops, e-learning courses, onsite training, and speakers. Also, forums operate in several subject areas of finance management in which participants can share job-specific content. Because the financial climate is so complex, finance managers in health care facilities need fairly frequent updating on policy and rule changes. And when the system is completely altered, as it will be in the near future, finance managers

INTERVIEW

Managing the Physician Network

Robert Goldstein, FACMPE

Executive Vice President for the New Physician Network, Moses Cone Health System, Greensboro, North Carolina

How did you get into the health care management field?

I was a premed major in undergraduate school, but realized I did not have the grades to get into medical or dental schools. I accidentally ran into an old fraternity brother who told me about a field that a lot of people did not know about—health administration. I thought that sounded interesting because my father was a businessman, and I had dabbled in that side of things. I had an interest in the scientific or medical side as well. I was lucky enough to be admitted to Duke where I pursued an MHA [master's in hospital administration]. When I graduated, I realized I had little experience, so I made the decision to do a postgraduate residency in an outpatient setting. I competed for and was fortunate to obtain a residency at the Ochsner Clinic in New Orleans, a large multispecialty practice. I then became an assistant clinic manager in a large group practice of over 120 MDs in Pensacola, Florida. It turned out to be a COO [chief operating officer] position, and I gained a great deal of experience working closely with various medical specialties, the operational areas, and was afforded vast latitude and freedom to learn the craft. After eight years, I went back to the Ochsner Clinic, where I remained for six years as associate administrator over various departments and functions. I [then] felt it was time to advance to a CEO or other senior position. I took a job with a 35-plus multispecialty group practice in New Orleans where I stayed for 12 years. We did a lot of innovative work at that practice, and we were heavily involved in capitation and managed care. In 2002, I came to Greensboro to work at the Moses Cone Health System as vice president. My responsibility was overseeing the overall functioning of LeBauer Health Care. In 2008, I was promoted to Executive Vice President for the new Physician Network division and I also retained responsibility as Vice President for LeBauer.

Why do you think people choose group practice administration?

People may choose group practice administration because you can exercise more autonomy and more entrepreneurial initiatives. There may be a sense that there is less hierarchy and bureaucracy compared to a hospital setting. The vast majority of people who are practice managers, I believe, find running physician offices very similar to running a small or medium-sized business. There are many opportunities, and often there are challenges. One is constrained by regulations to be sure, but I believe this field allows one to be creative and innovative. At the end of the day, an indicator of success for the practice manager is how much the physicians get paid. Ultimately it is up to the practice manager to oversee the practice and provide an environment in which both physicians and patients thrive.

Why is it advantageous for group practices to be part of a large health system, and how does it affect administrators?

The whole process of hospitals acquiring physician practices has gone through a cyclical history. In the late 1980s and 90s there was a flurry of hospitals that rushed to purchase physician practices. This was done in order to secure a primary care base and a referral base. Many times, several hospitals competed with each other in order to maintain their current book of business or increase their market share. During that period, in addition to hospitals, hospital companies, or health system acquisitions, there were a few proprietary firms who also purchased practices thinking that they could increase their margin through economies of scale and enhancing ancillaries. This proprietary approach essentially failed because there was only so much you [could] squeeze out of the practice without ultimately affecting the physician's compensation. As to the hospital or system approach, in the flurry to accomplish the task of employing physicians, no thought was given to any sort of productivity requirement and compensation was not tied to work. Therefore, a physician might be offered a salary of X dollars a year with no requirement to tie salary to performance. Thus, in many cases, doctors moved from more productive to less productive schedules. Ultimately, hospitals lost on that model and divested.

Now, the industry is moving to a model where physicians' practices are absorbed by hospitals and health systems. This time, health systems and hospitals are not paying for practices; the days of paying for good will and discounted cash flow for the practice are gone. Physician practices are still attractive to hospitals because most community hospitals recognize and feel responsible for community need—maintaining a certain level of medical specialties in the area and, of course, maintaining an active medical staff that supports the facility. The advantage to the group practice of being part of a large system is that hospitals and health systems often obtain better third-party payer

(continues on next page)

INTERVIEW

Managing the Physician Network (continued)

contracts. They can demand more well managed care and commercial contracts with insurers than solo physician practices.

How would you characterize your relationship with the physicians in your practice?
I am a physician advocate. After 30 plus years of working for and with doctors, I have to be. In my current position, I have to also remain loyal and be a part of the larger system. So essentially I have to be accountable to the physicians and the health system bosses. As a practice administrator, you also have a responsibility to the patients and to work with the physicians to focus on patient care.

How would you assess career opportunities in health care management?
Health administration has always been a fertile field. Generally speaking, it is not a well-known field. People still do not know how you get to be a health care administrator. There are great opportunities in a wide variety of areas. Things have developed since the mid-1970s when I started, and [when] it seemed that the only areas of concentration might have been marketing, planning, finance, and operations. Health care is developing from a cottage industry to one that is more mainstream. This opens up greater opportunity for specialization. Also, just prior to the recent economic downturn other industry sectors were not changing as fast as health care, particularly in reference to changing legislation and regulations. For instance, take the change that will probably occur around bundling of service payments. In the future, one payment will cover both the inpatient stay and the physicians' charges. That will probably create a new avenue for financial

will have a whole new fiduciary system to master and integrate into their institutions.

Credentialing: The designations of Certified Health care Financial Professional (CHFP) and Fellow of the Health care Financial folks to specialize in. As the population ages and medicine continues to advance, there will be in my opinion an ever-increasing need for well-trained health care professionals.

What do you see as future trends in the industry?
One is specialization of roles. There will be a continued focus on expertise, background, and education. Health care will continue to move into the mainstream in terms of operating from a management perspective, like other industries do. Integration of clinical roles and management roles will also increase. Individuals with a background in a clinical area—for instance, nursing and management—will be a highly valued commodity. We will experience a need for folks to be trained in quality measurement and related fields; for instance, in six sigma [a quality management strategy], with an ability to measure productivity in the workplace and relate to improved outcomes and the efficient use of all resources. In terms of practice management, there will continue to be an emphasis on individuals who are well trained in the physician-office setting.

How would you describe the latest trends in technology?
I think of technology in two broad categories. First is the technology related to the provision of health services; for instance, MRI (magnetic resonance imaging), lab-testing equipment, equipment you can provide for an ambulatory surgery unit, scopes for colonoscopies—anything physicians can provide to patients that will generate a return. Is it an improvement? Is it a clinical enhancement? Is it a good investment? Even if it is not a good investment, will it provide better patient care? Do I need more staff to run a new system? All of these questions need to be asked.

Second is the major impact of the electronic medical record. The big change that will affect group practices significantly will be moving from a paper to an electronic chart. In four years, virtually all physician offices will have to have electronic charts or else it will affect reimbursement. This will also have a major positive effect on patient care and outcomes.

Management Association (FHFMA) help prepare health care finance professionals for increasingly responsible positions in the health care industry; obtaining the credential helps financial management executives demonstrate a dedication to professional development. Also, a Credentialed Revenue Cycle Representative (CRCR), which designates proficiency in the revenue cycle field, can be earned through a self-study course and an exam.

Career Services: There are several publications published by the organization that deal with career issues, as well as information on the Web site that offers specific career advice directed toward early careerists and students. HFMA also operates a job bank for seekers, employers, and recruiters.

Advocacy: HFMA members often testify before the House Financial Services Committee on issues concerning the financial health of their institutions. In May, 2009, HFMA member Michael M. Allen, CFO of Winona Health, presented testimony on behalf of HFMA before the U.S. House Financial Services Committee. The testimony addressed the impact of recent municipal bond financing issues on not-for-profit hospitals.

Healthcare Information Management Systems Society (HIMSS)

HIMSS is the health care industry's membership organization exclusively focused on providing leadership for the optimal use of health care information technology (IT) and management systems for the betterment of health care. It has 350 corporate members and over 20,000 individual members. There are chapters in the United States, Europe, the Middle East, and Asia.

Conferences: Highlights of the annual meeting are the more than 900 vendors who showcase their latest health care innovations, more than 300 educational sessions, and the national and international networking opportunities. A big issue in 2009 and going forward is the role of this organization in computerizing electronic health records, which has been called for by President Obama. A keynote speaker in the 2009 conference was Alan Greenspan, who addressed industry issues of patient safety, health care costs, and privacy and security. Global conferences are also held for international members.

Education: Online learning is provided in several relevant areas through Webinars, audio conferencing, and other distance education programs. One Webinar series deals with the IT aspects of the new legislation enacted by Congress, the American Recovery and Reinvestment Act of 2009, which includes $19.2 billion in provisions for health care IT technology.

Everyone

Knows

Social Insurance

There are three major players in the social insurance area, which provide access to health care for different population groups. They are Medicare, Medicaid, and the federal entitlement programs for veterans.

Medicare. This federal program provides health care coverage for those over 65, for permanently disabled adults, and for those suffering from end-stage renal disease. Part A is the hospital benefit, Part B covers outpatient visits and preventive services, Part C are the Medicare Choice plans that extend Medicare benefits, and Part D is the prescription drug benefit. Medicare expenditures are increasing dramatically as the population ages and the cost of care rises.

Medicaid. After Medicare, Medicaid is the second largest provider of social health insurance in the United States. It is provided for the medically indigent and is jointly funded by the federal government and individual states. States have significant autonomy in administering benefits, and these benefits can differ dramatically from state-to-state. Federal and state governments have been active in applying cost controls as Medicaid costs escalate.

Insuring Members and Families of the Military. The Department of Defense has 536 hospitals and clinics worldwide and is part of TRICARE, the military health program, which covers active duty personnel, retired personnel, and families. The Veterans Health Administration operates the nation's largest health care system with 160 medical centers and 1,000 community clinics, and all veterans are eligible for services.

Credentialing: Individuals who meet eligibility criteria and successfully complete the CPHIMS exam are designated a Certified Professional in Health care Information and Management Systems (CPHIMS).

Career Services: The job board operates for seekers, employers, and recruiters. A few of the jobs listed on the board in June 2009 were for a quality assurance manager, supervisor of medical records coding, data analyst, and consultant in health care software. Career development resources are available in abundance on the Web site and include information on interviewing, résumés, networking, and articles on much more.

Advocacy: The Society does not employ a registered lobbyist, but they sponsor specific activities like HIMSS annual national Advocacy Day in which nearly 300 HIMSS individual members meet with their elected members of Congress to press for issues that are of concern—like computerizing medical records.

Medical Group Management Association (MGMA)

MGMA is the principal voice for medical group practice administrators. Its membership comprises CEOs, physician managers, board members, office members, and other management professionals who work in large and small group practices, practices as part of hospital systems, and ambulatory care organizations. According to Robert Goldstein, "MGMA provides a vast amount of information in a number of ways. They have 22,000 members, representing 150,000 physicians. MGMA has a professional side that provides a fellowship track through ACMPE, American College of Medical Practice Executives."

Conferences: The MGMA Annual Conference is the largest professional development and networking conference for medical practice administrators. Over a period of four days, it includes general sessions by established speakers, chapter get-togethers, career sessions, and plenty of opportunities for networking.

Education: The organization offers national conferences, a leadership seminar series, online education, seminars, and Webinars on such subjects as "Road Map to a Better Performing Practice," "Evaluating the Financial Health of Your Practice," and "Health Care Compliance." The Core Learning Series covers a variety of domains through the publication entitled *A Body of Knowledge* that supplies all of the information needed to master the competencies in this field.

Credentialing: You can become board certified and earn a CMPE—Certified Medical Practice Executive—through the American College of Medical Practice Executives (ACMPE, the standard-setting and certification body of MGMA) after completing required classroom hours, supplying references, and so forth. The designation of Fellow, which is the highest designation that can be earned as a practice manager, can be achieved after receiving the CMPE and writing several papers and case studies and fulfilling other criteria.

Career Services: These are extensive and include books and surveys, education resources that include an "MGMA Boot Camp" online course, tools and research, a medical job board, and online career-related articles written by fellow members. In May 2009, there were 573 jobs posted to the job board, attesting to the vigor of the industry even in difficult times.

Advocacy: MGMA maintains a Government Affairs staff that informs members of the latest issues and policy decisions affecting health care management. A few of the issues at play are the Medicare physician fee schedule, Physician Quality Reporting Initiative, and Medicare billing.

National Center for Healthcare Leadership (NCHL)

NCHL is a not-for-profit organization that works to assure that high-quality, relevant, and responsible leadership is available to meet the challenges of delivering quality patient health care in the 21st century. NCHL's goal is to improve health system performance and the health status of the entire country through effective health care management leadership. With important linkages to the largest hospitals, hospital systems, and other health care facilities across the county NCHL is the industry's "go-to" place for specific information and training related to the leadership issues of health care administrators today. They run several programs in pursuit of leadership excellence: Leadership Excellence Network (LENS), Health Demonstration Project, Nurse Team Leadership Project, and University Graduate Health Demonstration Project. NCHL, as a leadership organization for health care managers, interacts and advises all of the organizations listed above and the many other professional groups associated with the industry.

Chapter 3

On the Job

Health care managers perform a variety of functions in multiple set-tings. One who seeks a career in the health care management field could have the education and skills of a lawyer, a health care clini-cian, a marketing or public relations professional, a policy analyst, a financial analyst, an academician, a managerial consultant, a lead-ership expert, a nursing home administrator, or be adept in many other areas of expertise. Cynthia Haddock notes that the health ser-vices administration is not an industry but a set of occupations, and it also encompasses a broad range of industries, noting that "a single integrated health care system might include subsidiaries in indus-tries as diverse as durable medical equipment sales, medical care services, and long-term care services."

This chapter provides a clearer view of the extremely broad land-scape of choices for those who wish to enter the health care man-agement field. Included here are job capsules that provide basic job information and educational requirements. For ease of organization, the occupations described in the capsules are sorted into six set-tings—academic and public health, consultants, hospitals, insurance, medical group practices, and military and long-term care facilities.

Most health administration jobs are in clinical settings, so let us take a look at the major ones. Every job in health management or administration is related in some way to the delivery of services in the following nine segments. The descriptions are adapted from Beaufort Longest and Kurt Darr, writing in their 2008 book, *Manag-ing Health Services Organizations and Systems*.

(1) *Hospitals.* Hospitals cover the full range of medical care, ranging from diagnostic services to surgery and continuous nursing care. Care may be provided overnight on an inpatient basis or on an outpatient basis in a clinic or other hospital facility. A trend in recent years is for hospital care to shift from an inpatient to outpatient basis when possible. Many hospitals are part of larger health systems that include long-term care facilities, group practices, lab facilities, and more. Tim Rice, the author of the Foreword of this book, is president and CEO of such a system. The hospital is where one can see almost the full range of occupations for the administrator—from the CEO, to finance and marketing staff, to admitting personnel, to IT staff.

(2) *Nursing and Residential Care Facilities.* These facilities provide inpatient nursing, rehabilitation, and health-related personal care for those requiring continuous care but not necessarily hospital services. Convalescent homes help patients who need fewer services. Residential care facilities minister to children, the elderly, and those who have limited ability to care for themselves. Other settings where nursing and medical care are not the main functions include assisted-living facilities, alcohol and drug rehabilitation centers, group homes, and halfway houses. Nurse administrators are often found in residential care facilities, as well as art and recreation therapists, finance managers, and human resources staff.

(3) *Physician Offices.* About 37 percent of all health care establishments are physician practices. Doctors can practice solo or in twos or threes, but the trend has been to aggregate into large group practices of practitioners who have the same or a variety of specialties. Such an arrangement is beneficial for physicians because they afford backup coverage, reduce overhead expenses, facilitate consultation with peers, and position them more favorably in negotiations with insurance companies and other organizations. The physicians work as salaried employees, adding a whole new dimension to the job of administrator in such practices. The administrators perceive themselves as running a business, and are often on the front line in making those human resource and finance decisions that in a hospital setting would be handled by a staff. Many administrators see this as a positive, as they can be entrepreneurs without the hospital's bureaucracy.

(4) *Dentist Offices.* About one out of every five health care establishments is a dental office. There are many more solo practitioners

in this area, and in these offices there will usually only be a dentist, an office manager, and one or two other employees. There are also group practices that may combine general dentists and dental surgeons. These larger offices will have administrators and a staff closer to the group practice model for physicians.

(5) *Home Services.* Skilled nursing or medical care is sometimes provided in the home under a physician's indirect supervision. These services are for the elderly as well as anyone else who needs maintenance but not necessarily inpatient care. Such services as infusion therapy, chemotherapy, pain management, dietary support, and respiratory therapy are offered. Nurses, occupational therapists, dieticians, social workers, and many others are part of their clinical staffs. With the preference of many to be treated at home when possible, this part of the health care industry is growing quite fast and needing many more people in management positions.

(6) *Offices of Other Health Practitioners.* Hospital and other health facilities often contract out for chiropractors, optometrists, podiatrists, occupational and physical therapists, psychologists, audiologists, speech-language pathologists, dieticians, and other health practitioners. These are very often solo practices that may require a medical secretary or bookkeeper, However, there are some aggregate practices that are structured similarly to group practices in their administrative structure and needs.

(7) *Outpatient Care Centers.* Kidney dialysis centers, outpatient mental health and substance abuse centers, health maintenance organization medical centers, and ambulatory surgical and medical centers are examples of outpatient care centers. Typically, generalist administrators with the titles of senior administrator or assistant administrator are found in these organizations with less emphasis on the subspecialties like marketing and public relations.

(8) *Other Ambulatory Health Care Services.* You do not hear much about this segment, but there is a place in the health care spectrum for ambulance and helicopter services, blood and organ banks, and other ambulatory health care services like pacemaker monitoring services. Obviously, the business of these organizations lies in coordinating with other health care facilities. This is a small subspecialty for occupations, but they are considered a vital segment. There is even a professional organization for these individuals—the National Association of Healthcare Transportation Management (NAHTM).

(9) *Medical and Diagnostic Laboratories.* These laboratories provide diagnostic or analytic information to the medical profession and directly to patients. Workers are lab technicians, tomographers, and others who perform clinical tests. This is the smallest segment with the fewest workers and the fewest administrators.

Academic and Public Health Careers

Though not typically thought of as being in the arena of health care management or administration, there are many occupations here that apply. Universities, colleges, and community colleges have programs that relate to health care administration and to public health issues. There are opportunities for instructors, researchers, and educators at all levels, especially since the United States is placing a high priority on building up the nation's public health workforce. Research institutes, government aid organizations, and nonprofits also hire public health professionals. Since 2002, federal funding has increased for public health preparedness and includes scholarships and loans for those wishing to enter the field. The jobs themselves run the gamut of community health educator to professors in degreed programs. Here is a look at some of them.

Biostatistician

Biostatistics is the science that applies statistical theory and mathematical principles to research in medicine, biology, environmental science, public health, and related fields. Public health biostatisticians use mathematical and scientific methods to determine the cause of disease and injuries and to identify health trends within communities. For instance, if you go into this career your research may include estimating the number of deaths from gun violence or determining trends in drunk-driving injuries. It may also include analyzing the effectiveness of new drugs, analyzing risk factors for different illnesses, planning health care interventions, and explaining biological phenomena. If you like collecting and studying information, forecasting scenarios, and drawing conclusions, this may be the perfect health career for you. Positions are available in data management, pharmaceutical and clinical trials, and in academia. At least a master's degree in biostatistics is required from a school of public health.

Community Health Worker

Community health workers (CHWs) are frontline public health workers who have an intimate understanding of the community they serve. CHWs engage in a range of activities including outreach,

Professional
Ethics

Medical Ethics

In a survey of *Harvard Business Review* subscribers (http://harvardbusinessonline.hbsp.harvard.edu), many of the ethical dilemmas reported by health care managers involved conflicts with superiors, customers, and subordinates. The most frequent issues involved dishonesty in communication with top management, clients, and government agencies. Significantly, managers' bosses were singled out as sometimes pressuring their subordinates to engage in such unethical activities as supporting incorrect viewpoints, signing false documents, overlooking the boss's wrongdoings, and doing business with the boss's friends.

Obviously, these ethical problems extend beyond the field of health care management. However, according to Donald Lombardi and John Schermerhorn (2007) the health care industry has its own set of ethical considerations:

- *Care.* Whether you are processing insurance claims or preparing a patient for knee surgery, care means providing health services to patients that shows that you are interested in his or her best health outcome.

- *Concern.* Staff should show concern not only to patients and their physical, emotional, and mental well-being but also to each other.

- *Compassion.* This is critical to have at all levels of health care organizations, whether you are interacting with patients or coworkers.

- *Community.* A feeling of unity within a department, area, or the whole facility is helpful in furthering a positive outcome for patients.

- *Confidentiality.* Know when to share information—there are appropriate times for this—and when to abide by the federal and state laws and organizational guidelines and protect patients' privacy.

community education, informal counseling, and social support and advocacy in order to build health knowledge. CHWs can be found in many geographic and demographic settings, but are most often found in underserved areas where they can serve as a bridge between the community and the health care, government, and social service systems. Community health workers help people access local health systems more efficiently, help them understand their own health needs and what to do about them, act as a cultural arbiter between their world and the world of health distribution, advocate for local health needs, and perform many other functions. They can go by a variety of names that include community health advisor, family advocate, health educator, liaison, promoter, outreach worker, peer counselor, patient navigator, health interpreter, and public health aide. A bachelor's degree in health sciences is the minimum requirement for this occupation.

Environmental Health Advocate

Environmental health advocates are public health officials who work to identify potential threats to public health, increase awareness about the situation, and give people the facts they need to protect their health. Advocates partner with health care professionals to establish health guidelines, which they then promote through local, state, and national awareness campaigns. Environmental health advocates can be specialists in infectious diseases, epidemiology, statistics, or communication; their work includes identifying viruses that threaten the public, such as the "swine" flu strain that emerged in 2009. They also might be responsible for such tasks as distributing mosquito nets to people in remote malaria-ridden areas and vaccinating children against preventable diseases. Environmental health advocates work for local, state, and government agencies, consulting firms, and nonprofit organizations. They may travel domestically or internationally to attend meetings and make presentations. Because this job requires interaction with many different types of people and organizations, good written and communication skills are necessary. Flexibility is also an asset, as travel and new challenges may arise at any moment. At minimum, a bachelor's degree in either a science or communication major is necessary. Some states certify environmental health scientists, and many of them hold master's degrees in environmental health science.

Global Health Professional

International/global health is an area of public health that addresses the health of people living in developing countries. Health concerns in these countries include not only infectious and tropical diseases (such as HIV/AIDS, tuberculosis, sexually transmitted diseases, and malaria), but also chronic and non-infectious diseases, as well as age-related illnesses and conditions. Global health also addresses maternal and child health, mental illness, and the health consequences of trauma, violence, war, and displacement. Another focus of the global health professional is the organization, financing, and management of health service systems. Some of the settings where global health specialists find themselves are in disaster relief organizations, research and academic institutions, non-governmental agencies, and government organizations. A master's degree in public health is required with an emphasis in the area of global health. This may include courses in coping with complex emergencies, health care financing, population policy, and others.

Health Sociologist

Health sociologists identify and explain the influence of social factors on health and health care. They conduct research on how social factors affect the incidence and course of disease, on how patients and the general population respond to various health conditions, and on the acceptance and rejection of specific treatments. Sociologists gather data and look for common social values and behavior and attitudinal orientations. This data helps to identify trends on why people seek medical attention, how they cope with terminal illness, how practitioners behave, and more. Health sociologists were part of the research team that discovered the first cluster of AIDS. They documented the spread of AIDS and have for the last several years studied patterns of behavior of risk groups. Health sociologists work in universities, for federal health agencies, in state and local health departments, in major hospitals and research institutes, and in professional schools. A Ph.D., while not required, enhances the range of employment opportunities. Personal characteristics that lead to success in the field are inquisitiveness, strong speaking and writing skills, analytic skills, objectivity, and perseverance. The field is growing, especially for social gerontologists who study the special problems faced by the aged.

Health Educator

This individual helps improve public health by encouraging people to make positive health choices. Health educators develop community-wide education initiatives on health topics ranging from nutrition and fitness to injury and disease prevention. They also can include programs geared to stop the spread of sexually transmitted diseases, to help young people recognize and avoid the dangers of alcohol and drug abuse, to participate in developing programs to reduce obesity, and to improve the quality of life for seniors. Research is also part of this job, and many health educators conduct studies that facilitate better access to health services, better self-care practices, and a community's active participation in available health systems. A degree in behavioral science or health education is required from a school of public health.

Medical Historian

The history of medicine is a small and specialized branch of history. Medical historians commonly teach in universities, either in the history department or the medical school. They also may teach within the health fields, depending upon their training and expertise. Medical historians also work in museums with historical medical collections (e.g., the Smithsonian's National Museum of American History), or in libraries and archives that specialize in medical history (e.g., the National Library of Medicine). They develop public exhibits, organize and provide access to historical collections, and carry out research leading to scholarly publications in the field. Virtually all medical history positions involve some degree of library research. Most historians require a doctorate in history or in the history of medicine or science. Some medical historians are physicians who also have degrees in history.

Nurse Educator

The newspapers and other media have been full of reports describing a nursing shortage, yet there are plenty of candidates for nursing schools. The problem is that there are not enough nurse educators to staff the educational institutions; in fact, according to the August 15, 2008, edition of the *St. Louis Business Journal*, 40,000 nursing candidates were turned away in the academic year 2007–08. Nurse educators are registered nurses with advanced education who are also teachers. Most work as nurses for a period of time before dedicating their careers to educating future nurses. Nurse educators serve as faculty members in nursing schools and teaching hospitals. They develop lesson plans, teach courses, evaluate educational programs, oversee students' clinical practice, and serve as role models for their students. They may teach general courses or focus on areas of specialization such as geriatric nursing, pediatric nursing, or nursing informatics. With experience, nurse educators may advance to administrative roles, managing nurse education programs, writing or reviewing textbooks, and developing continuing education. Most nurse educators complete a master's degree in nursing (some universities require a doctorate); all, of course, are registered nurses with a valid license and several years of experience.

Professor of Health Administration

There are many undergraduate and graduate programs in health administration. Professors are usually experienced in the field, either through having worked as administrators or having had a medical background before turning to administration. They teach courses in management, financial management of health care institutions, health policy, informational technology specific to health care, and other subjects directly related to managing in a health care setting. In graduate programs, professors usually hold a Ph.D., or an MBA or MHA. An academic career is often a logical and preferred step for many experienced health care managers at mid- or late career.

Reproductive Health Specialist

Aspiring professionals can follow the medical, educational, or policy route to prepare for this position. The medical route might involve working in health care clinics run by community groups or nongovernmental organizations. The educational route can include study at medical, pharmacy, and nursing schools, or schools of public health. Those who go into the policy aspects of the field are often employed by such organizations as the World Health Organization (WHO) and the United Nations Population Fund. The specific role of the reproductive specialist depends on the area of focus, but he or she is most often involved in providing education and referral services about family planning and reproductive health. A master's in public health is required, which can be combined with a degree in nursing, pharmacy, or medicine.

Consultants

Health care is an expensive and highly regulated business covering a wide variety of administrative functions. It is inevitable that a need would arise for people with expertise to help health care organizations grow, prosper, and fend off potential obstacles. Consultants fulfill needs in organizations that do not have individuals on staff who possess specialized areas of expertise. Because the breadth of the health care industry is so extensive, consultants specialize in many areas—insurance, leadership, management, start-up expertise, legal, finance, and others. They require high-level skills such as knowledge of accounting, information systems, organizational behavior, and communications.

Hospital and Health Care Facility Consultant

These consultants serve specialty hospitals, health delivery systems, and health care management companies. Consultants provide services that include the preparation of marketing analyses, business planning, strategic reorganization, acquisitions, start-ups, turnarounds (helping failing health organizations renew themselves), and service-line development (instituting a patient-focused view of key business lines). Some consultants in this area also provide executive search, interim management, and related consulting. They engage in activities such as market research, salary surveys, marketing planning, competitive analyses, and business development to support their recommendations and work with senior-level managers in health care settings. Consultants in this area may be former clinicians with wide experience in the areas within which they consult.

Legal Nurse Consultant

These are nurses who assist attorneys in legal cases that involve medical issues. Legal nurse consultants, or LNCs, are employed by law firms, hospitals, insurance companies, government agencies, and consulting firms, and many are self-employed. LNCs evaluate, analyze, and render informed opinions on the delivery of health care in any a number of areas or situations. They assist in obtaining the appropriate medical records that apply to a case, they help determine the merits of the case, prepare a chronology of events, conduct research, assist with depositions, and act as a liaison between physicians, attorneys, and clients. In short, the LNC uses his or her medical knowledge to help legal staff advance a case in the areas of malpractice, personal injury, disability, risk management, and more. LNCs need to be up-to-date on their health care and legal knowledge, have good communication skills, and be detail-oriented. An RN (registered nurse) is required, and certification—Legal Nurse Consultant Certified (LNCC)—can be obtained through the process offered by the American Association of Legal Nurse Consultants (AALNC).

Marketing Consultant

The primary task of the marketing consultant is to provide the most appropriate and beneficial marketing strategies to medical practices, hospitals, and other integrated systems. The job requires familiarity with the community resources available for promotion, as well as good outreach and networking skills. This person has usually had extensive experience in a hospital or practice setting, sometimes in a variety of administrative jobs. Or, the individual may be a marketing expert who has channeled his or her expertise through the health care setting. At minimum, a bachelor's degree is required. It is helpful to possess a MHA, an MPH, or advanced degree in marketing and communications.

Practice Consultant

Medical practices, large and small, usually require some help in getting their organizations started and keeping them financially viable while maintaining quality delivery of care. This consultant provides financial analysis and benchmarking tools, state-of-the-art IT resources, and field-tested deliverables. Diagnostics are part of the package of services that can reveal the strengths and weaknesses of practice management and provide a basis for recommendations. Practice consultants do chart reviews (ensuring compliance with coding practices and that codes are up-to-date) and site evaluations that check for compliance with OSHA and HIPAA regulations. They also review accounts receivable systems, negotiate with insurance companies for contracts, conduct fee analyses, develop personnel policies, and conduct a general review of financial aspects, which are benchmarked with the recommendations from the Medical Group Management Association (MGMA). Practice consultants fill in areas of information and technical expertise that are not provided by existing staff in the medical group.

Senior Care Consultant

In this type of consulting, the individual offers insight and guidance at both the strategic and operational levels to help clients—hospitals or senior care facilities—to build market share, improve organizational efficiencies, manage declining reimbursement rates, and comply with regulatory changes. Some legal experience and an MBA, MPH, or MHA is required.

Hospital Careers

The modern American hospital is a wondrous place, full of technological innovations and sophisticated management systems and equipment. If you look at hospitals as social and economic systems, there are jobs that cut across the spectrum, from senior administrator to public relations professionals. The wide array of administrative jobs presented here are also found in other settings, such as group practices or long-term care facilities.

Administrator

This is a generic term that can cover most of the jobs listed below or can describe a specific function as general administrator, which can include titles such as assistant administrator, administrator, senior administrator, vice-president, president, and CEO.

Assistant Administrator

Large facilities usually have several assistant administrators who aid the top administrator and handle daily decisions. Assistant administrators direct activities in clinical areas such as nursing, surgery, therapy, medical records, or health information. Administrators are often are responsible for facilities and equipment worth millions of dollars, and for hundreds of employees. To make effective decisions, they need to be open to different opinions and good at analyzing contradictory information. They must understand finance and information systems and be able to interpret data. Motivating others to implement their decisions requires strong leadership abilities. Tact, diplomacy, flexibility, and communication skills are essential because medical and health services managers spend most of their time interacting with others. A degree in hospital administration or a combined degree is necessary for advancement. Assistant administrators advance by moving into more responsible and higher paying positions, such as associate administrator, department head, or chief executive officer, or by moving to larger facilities. Some experienced managers also may become consultants or professors of health care management. New graduates with master's degrees in health services administration may start as department managers or as supervisory staff.

Chief Executive Officer

The person in this role can also be called executive director, executive vice president, or president. Because the CEO is responsible for all aspects of a hospital's daily operations and division functions, the CEO's desk is where the buck stops. In some large hospital centers, the CEO is like a mayor of a small city who leads, innovates, builds systems beneficial to the organization, runs interference, manages crises, and protects the population—in this case, both patients and employees. Tim Rice, the author of the Foreword of this book, is the CEO of a large hospital system that includes several hospitals, ambulatory care centers, laboratories, and several ancillary services. The CEO is responsible for adherence to the hospital's mission. He or she also develops and implements strategic plans for maintaining and improving delivery of services. The CEO works closely with medical staff and relies on their judgment in patient care matters. At this level, a graduate degree in hospital administration is generally required. It is usually the function of the board of trustees to hire a competent and highly skilled person for this position.

Admitting Manager

Admitting personnel are responsible for explaining the procedure of admittance to patients. This individual supervises and trains admitting clerks to perform the functions of admitting, which include

Best
Practice

The Influence of the Health Care Executive

Health care executives are typically highly respected members of their communities and are frequently called on to head boards, run for office, and take senior positions in local government. Hospitals and health care organizations are often the largest employers in many areas, and their organizations positively impact the health of the populations they serve and the well-being of the entire community. For example, Tim Rice, CEO of Moses Cone Health System in Greensboro, North Carolina, which employs nearly 7,500 people, is serving a term as head of the city's Chamber of Commerce.

assigning the patient a room, notifying other hospital departments of the admission, and taking all of the administrative and clerical data needed for the patient's record. The admitting staff also explains the rules and procedures of the institution and obtains signatures on release and permission forms. The manager is in charge of supervising and coordinating all departmental functions. A degree in business administration or social science is required. For the manager's position, a few years of prior experience in an admitting function is necessary.

Controller

The controller is the head of the fiscal division of the hospital and is responsible for the entire area of financial management including budgeting, bookkeeping, general accounting, crediting, and collections. The controller usually reports to the hospital administrator and financial department heads—business office manager, accountant, and patient accounts manager—report to the controller. The controller has to know how the hospital runs as a business so that the administrative decisions about appropriate fees can be carried out. Financial management in a hospital is different in the sense that some institutions are nonprofit organizations (of the 3,900 acute care hospitals in the United States, 62 percent are considered nonprofit), so traditional business systems are not always used and controllers are often called upon to innovate new systems. Controllers work closely with the many hospital department managers in the course of the job's duties in order to work out ways to improve their fiscal operations. Minimum educational requirements include a bachelor's degree in accounting or business administration. Some hospitals require state certification as a certified public accountant. Controllers are often promoted from the position of senior accountant or business office manager.

Data Processing Manager

Information technology is an essential service in the hospital community. Patient charts, medical tests, financial records, and many other functions must be accurately and efficiently managed for a hospital to call itself well run. The data processing manager coordinates the many systems that comprise a hospital's information system. He or she is responsible for planning, programming, and processing of data and information. A major task of this manager is to advise management on new information systems and to inform department heads about financial and statistical reports that are generated. Experience in programming and systems work is helpful, and several years' experience in computer-related work is required. A bachelor's degree in computer science, accounting, or mathematics is essential.

Director of Hospital Fund-raising and Development

The director develops programs to raise money to cover both non-reimbursed and capital expenditures of nonprofit hospitals. This role is essential because nonprofit hospitals need to augment their revenues from third-party providers and patients. This individual is responsible for planning fund-raising activities like dinners, auctions, and balls; developing annual giving programs; approaching corporations and individuals for gifts; seeking out grants; and planning direct-mail campaigns. Also part of the job is attending events on behalf of the institution, speaking to groups, and providing tours and other services to donors. A great deal of writing is in involved, as these directors are responsible for developing direct mail letters, written appeals for bequests, brochures, press releases, advertisement copy, and fund-raising letters. Working with public relations and marketing, volunteers, and sometimes board members is usually required. The director is responsible for supervising and training subordinate staff and is also responsible for maintaining donor records and preparing budgets. Employment prospects are fair—not every institution has this position since it is limited to nonprofit hospitals, extended care facilities, nursing homes, and other health care organizations. A person who is in this position can advance by going to a larger system or by becoming head of hospital marketing or public relations. A bachelor's degree is required with possible majors in public relations, marketing, health care administration, journalism, and communication.

Director of Human Resources (HR)

This department head is responsible for many of the traditional duties of the human resources director in many institutions. That is, he or she oversees recruitment, selection, and placement of employees within the medical center. HR directors also develop personnel policies and procedures on working conditions, employment practices, pay scales, and grievance procedures. Directors in hospitals have some further responsibilities with respect to appropriate employee behavior. For instance, when ward clerks are faced with anxious relatives of patients, that clerk must be trained to deal professionally and compassionately with the relatives' concerns. A bachelor's degree with a major in business administration, personnel administration, or industrial relations is required and a master's degree in personnel management is desirable.

Director of Managed Care

Managed care describes the techniques used to lower the cost of health care and to improve its quality. This is mostly done through provider networks that work together to negotiated cost-effective fees. The director coordinates the development of managed-care strategies and activities for a medical center and its affiliates, advising and consulting with operating departments to handle managed-care requirements such as utilization review, billing, and registration.

Solid knowledge of managed-care contracting requirements, various reimbursement models, and government regulations is required, and the ability to negotiate with physicians, vendors, and payers is desirable. Coordinating with practice groups and clinical departments on managed-care opportunities for specific programs such as employee assistance programs, occupational health, and substance abuse services is also part of this individual's job duties. At minimum, a bachelor's degree in business, finance, health care management, or a related field is required. An MPH, MHA, or MBA with a health care concentration is preferred.

Director of Marketing

This director is responsible for projects and tasks related to market research, planning, and promotion; interpretation of patient/customer/physician attitudes, values, and expectations; assessment of current programs; and testing of the clinical, operational, financial, ethical, medical, and legal feasibility of proposed programs. He or she evaluates trends in hospital usage, assesses the needs of the community, develops communication material, and prepares departmental budgets. The director works with the public relations staff and also makes sure hospital staff is aware of hospital services. Prospects for this position throughout the country are fair to good, with better opportunities in urban areas. A director can climb the career ladder by locating a similar position in a larger or more prestigious facility, and some strike out on their own as consultants. At least a bachelor's degree is required with several years of experience.

Director of Public Relations

The primary role of a person in this position is to promote a favorable public image for the facility. This individual is charged with putting together the most useful and illuminating information about the hospital and transmitting it to appropriate sources and venues. A hospital issues many nonscientific communications that inform the community about the hospital's activities and services, for which the director of public relations either takes personal responsibility or provides oversight for a staff. Also, part of the mission of this job is to organize and carry out special programs and activities such as health awareness events, child wellness sessions, and developing health support groups of various types. The director also prepares press releases that cover new departments or services being offered, physician activities and awards, new equipment being acquired, or changes to the physical facility, to name just a few. Coordination with both individuals in internal hospital departments and in external organizations, like newspapers and TV stations, is essential in this job. A bachelor's degree is required for any job in the public relations area. Degrees in journalism, communications, public relations, advertising and marketing, and English are good gateways into the field, and pursuing a master's in hospital administration is recommended. To advance to a director's position, additional experience is certainly required and often additional education as well.

Executive Housekeeper

As the director of the institution's housekeeping program, the manager must set the standards of cleanliness throughout the hospital. This function is obviously essential to patient well-being since infection and contagion are the scourges of hospitals that do not stay on top of sanitation standards. The manager establishes work methods and systems, prepares cleaning schedules, and hires and trains housekeepers. The hospital laundry may also fall under this person's area of responsibility. Knowledge of the hospital's operations and a thorough understanding of building materials and equipment are important. At minimum, a high school diploma is required and college courses in management are helpful.

Food Services Administrator

Hospitals have large kitchens that must serve both patients and staff. The food services administrator is the head dietician who directs and coordinates the food preparation for the entire hospital. This includes being responsible for the preparation of special diets for patients, whose recovery may depend on the quality and type of food being served. It also requires the administrator to develop menus that are appealing to both staff and patients. Morale can be enhanced by the quality of food preparation and presentation that is available. The manager also supervises personnel, requisitions food and supplies, and maintains records. Many food service managers have had experience with large-scale food operations like those found in universities. A degree in nutrition, business administration, or a related field is required.

Problem
Solving

Collaboration and Policy

John is a director of marketing in a large, integrated health care system and he has many people to supervise. Usually, this is an enjoyable task. John likes getting the message out about his health care system, and he enjoys mentoring subordinates on the best ways to do it. The fly in the ointment, though, is that there are two individuals who have been troublesome over the years. Rita, a marketing associate, and Barry, a market research analyst, are technically competent—that is why they are still around—but they generate complaints from patients and they cause problems for other staff. For instance, Rita recently worked up a marketing plan to encourage participation from the community in a new health initiative that one of the hospitals had established. She did not complete it until the last minute, though, and she had to call on the support staff and some of the public relations staff to stay late and help finish it up. Complaints reached John about Rita's habit of not planning her work more carefully. Barry, on the other hand, has alienated patients and clinical staff while doing surveys because of his gruff attitude and his expectation that they should drop everything and answer his questions.

John did not want to rock the boat. Both Rita and Barry had strong community ties as well as strong relationships with several of the physicians. John, realizing that they were still good contributors, did not want to alienate them. But the situation was at the crisis point, with staff and patients complaining.

John solved the problem by realizing that he was not serving the customer—the patient—in the best manner possible. He had lost sight of that value, and it was affecting his performance. John realized that he was not satisfied with "good enough." He instituted a program that created clear standards of service that applied to the whole department, including Rita and Barry. Through peer pressure, feedback, and measurement, John was able to improve performance standards for Rita and Barry and for the department as a whole.

Health Information Technician

The technician conducts health data collection, monitoring, maintenance, and reporting activities in accordance with established quality data principles, legal and regulatory standards, and best practice guidelines. Technicians monitor electronic and paper-based documentation through use of various electronic systems, and they support efforts to construct effective patient-record systems and a national health system information infrastructure. Common job titles include reimbursement specialist, information access and disclosure specialist, coder, medical records technician, data quality coordinator, supervisor, and more. In addition to hospitals, health information technicians may be found in group practices, insurance companies, public health departments, home health care agencies, and others. An associate's degree in a specific health care technician program is required.

Health Information Manager

There is a significant amount of paperwork, data, and information involved in patient care. A health information manager or administrator plans, develops, and supervises systems for the acquisition, analysis, retention, and retrieval of health records that are consistent with medical, administrative, ethical, and legal requirements of the particular health care delivery system. Their duties and scope of responsibilities depend on the size and type of institution. Some health information managers are in group practice settings as well. Their responsibilities include

- ➡ developing, analyzing, and evaluating health records
- ➡ supervising coding personnel
- ➡ analyzing patient and institutional data for program and research purposes
- ➡ developing in-service educational materials
- ➡ developing and implementing policies and procedures for processing medical legal documents and insurance
- ➡ designing information flow, data models, and definitions
- ➡ formulating strategic, functional, and user requirements for health information

A bachelor's degree in medical records administration or health information management is required. Three categories of HIM personnel are certified through the American Medical Records Association:

Registered Records Administrator

This person manages a records department, sets policies and procedures, supervises and trains records technicians, and works with medical staff and other personnel in hospital and medical centers.

Accredited Records Technician

The accredited records technician organizes and evaluates health information; compiles statistics; assigns medical code numbers; maintains various health record indexes; and manages the use, storage, and release of health information.

Certified Coding Specialist

The certified coding specialist (or certified professional coder) is a specialist in analyzing health records and assigning numerical codes used for reporting diagnoses and information for bill payment, Medicare and Medicaid categories, and others. Coding instruction can be found in community colleges throughout the country and also through courses offered by the American Academy of Professional Coders (AAPC). Those who acquire certification earn 28 percent more than non-credentialed coders.

Health Unit Coordinator

Health unit coordinators, or unit secretaries, assist in maintaining patient and unit records, ordering supplies, transcribing orders, coordinating patient activities for the unit, and serving as liaisons between staff, patients and visitors. They work in health care settings such as hospitals units, clinics, public health care agencies, or nursing homes. They serve as the communications link among departments, physicians, nursing staff, and patients and visitors. High school students should study health, computer courses, biology, and chemistry. Formal training is required, usually through a six-month to one-year program at a community or vocational-technical college. Individuals in this position can advance to higher administrative positions within the facility. Coordinators can achieve certification by completing coursework and taking an exam provided by the National Association of Health Unit Coordinators (NAHUC).

Health Promotion and Wellness Manager

This person assists the director of marketing, public relations, or program development in the design and implementation of health education and wellness activities. The coordinator promotes the health of people in the community served by the hospital. He or she does this by conducting research to determine community needs and by developing and implementing programs that will be beneficial for people. The programs may include health fairs, support groups for particular diseases, or social programs like those for teen mothers. Attending meetings and professional conferences is part of the job. The position may exist in large hospitals or hospital centers, but in smaller facilities public relations or marketing staff may perform these functions, making job prospects fair. Once in the position, opportunities for advancement include moving to a larger hospital, or advancing to director of health and wellness promotion or director of marketing or public relations, depending on education and experience. A bachelor's degree in nursing, health care, public relations, marketing, or communications is necessary, and experience in publicity or marketing is helpful.

Medical Librarian

These are information professionals who specialize in health resources and provide information for physicians, allied health professionals, patients, consumers, students, and corporations. In addition to hospitals, they are employed in academic medical centers, clinics, universities, professional schools, consumer health libraries, research centers, foundations, biotechnology centers, insurance companies, medical equipment manufacturers, pharmaceutical companies, publishers, the military, and government agencies. They help students pursuing degrees in health care, design Web sites, participate as members of research teams, and provide information to health care companies to help them develop new products and services. In administrative roles, they also serve as directors, chief information officers, and deans of information technology departments. A master's degree in library and information science is necessary, and undergraduate degrees in biology, medical sciences, management, and computer science are helpful.

Medical Social Worker

Medical and public health social workers provide psychosocial support to people, families, or vulnerable populations so they can cope with chronic, acute, or terminal illnesses such as Alzheimer's disease, cancer, or AIDS. They also advise family caregivers, counsel patients, and help plan for patients' needs after discharge from hospitals. They may arrange for at-home services, such as Meals-on-Wheels or home care. Some work on interdisciplinary teams that evaluate certain kinds of patients—geriatric or organ transplant patients, for example. Medical and public health social workers may work for hospitals, nursing and personal care facilities, individual and family services agencies, or local governments. A bachelor's degree (BSW) is required, with a master's degree in social work (MSW) preferred. The need for medical and public social workers is expected to grow 24 percent between the years 2006 and 2016.

Medical Transcriptionist

Transcriptionists are specialists in medical language and health care documentation. They interpret and transcribe dictation by physicians and other health professionals for patient assessments, workup procedures, clinical history, diagnoses, prognoses, and so on. They edit for grammar and clarity. In addition to hospitals, they can be found in group practices and other medical facilities. A high school degree is required at minimum. An RMT (registered medical transcriptionist) certification confers greater reliability and validity to the occupation and can be earned after completing coursework and passing an exam given by AHDI (Association for Healthcare Documentation Integrity).

Patient Advocate

The primary duties for this position are to handle patient problems and concerns, act as a liaison between patients and hospital administration and staff, and make staff aware of patients' perceptions of problems. The advocate is charged with coming up with a viable solution if there is a misunderstanding between the patient and staff. The advocate has to be skilled in identifying and assessing the problem, which may require interviewing hospital staff. The problems can include larger patient care problems or concerns, or something relatively simple like not having a working phone in the room. The solutions that advocates come up with can often forestall a dissatisfied patient taking legal action or going to the press. Advocates may also conduct surveys to assess patients' satisfaction with the hospital experience. Most hospitals and other health care facilities have at least one patient advocate on staff, and larger hospitals have more. Some patient advocates advance to supervisory positions in public relations departments. Because of the newness of this career, educational guidelines have not been well established. Most advocates have at least a two-year associate's degree, but generally a bachelor's degree is preferred.

Quality Assurance Director

This person monitors patient care, develops and implements programs to enhance patient care, supervises staff, and develops budgets. The purpose of a quality assurance department is to minimize risk to the facility that may lead to potential loss. The director must assess the current state of hospital programs and improve them or develop a new one that enhances patient care. This position usually oversees the utilization review (a process that monitors the use, delivery, and cost-effectiveness of medical services), including the evaluation of medical care, risk management, and staff reviews, in order to maintain high standards at the facility. The quality assurance director also makes sure there is compliance with federal and state agencies, the Joint Commission on the Accreditation of Healthcare Organizations, and third-party payers. The director also evaluates reviews by outside agencies of the hospital and recommends changes. He or she may also be responsible for handling communications with counsel on malpractice suits. Individuals in this field may be graduates of nursing schools or other clinical health care programs, they may have received training in medical records, or they have some form of a joint business and clinical degree.

Rehabilitation Counselor

Rehabilitation counselors help people who have been injured or disabled achieve the optimal functioning, given their disorder. The counselor first tests the patient for motor ability, skill level, and psychological makeup and then prepares a profile. This profile is used to consult with the patient's family and medical team in order to develop a rehabilitation plan that can include vocational and psychological counseling, occupational training, and various forms of physical and psychological therapy. The counselor provides support throughout the process. At a minimum, a bachelor's degree is required. Many rehabilitation counselors obtain master's degrees or doctorates, which prepares them for higher-level management positions in large hospital systems and other settings. Certification is offered by the Commission on Rehabilitation Counselor Certification (CRCC).

Insurance

Some individuals go from working in health care facilities to jobs in the insurance industry, and some go the other way. For instance in one career path, a physician worked as a clinician, then operated clinics and hospitals in Africa, then got a master's in health administration, worked in a group practice, and finally landed at an insurance company as an analyst.

Analyst in Contracting and Reimbursement

Duties include negotiating contracts with hospitals, physicians, and ancillary providers. This position also includes responsibility for developing fair and equitable reimbursement models for providers that ensure high-quality services for members and monitoring HMO performance in terms of utilization of services. Development and implementation of strategies for improved performance is part of the job. A challenge for individuals in these positions is to control health care costs in an environment where technology and variations in physician practice contribute to high expenditures. A bachelor's degree in business or finance is preferred.

Director of Account Management

The director of account management is a senior-level member of the organization who has full authority and responsibility for the strategic planning and management of all account management resources for the corporation. Specific duties include reviewing and evaluating all account management functions and assuring a uniform process;

leading the account management division in day-to-day operations; working collaboratively with the CEO, COO, and other senior executives on creating strategy and developing policies; directing yearly reporting tasks for the department; and assuring that procedures are in compliance with HIPAA and other regulatory requirements. The director interacts regularly with the company's sales team, customer service staff, IT staff, and with senior management. Leadership responsibilities like facilitating the flow of knowledge and ideas, overseeing the career development of staff, and developing and

Keeping
in Touch

Online Networking

Practice administrators can use the social networking sites to their advantage. Facebook pages are free, easy to set up, can strengthen the brand of the medical office or hospital, and give the administrator a new way to connect with patients outside their office visits and other traditional communication methods. Although some businesses view social networking as counterproductive and a time-waster, it can be an advantage to have designated employees conduct outreach on a practice's Facebook page. Facebook is not just a place to play, but can be a venue for connecting people with similar interests. When a practice creates a Facebook page, they create the ability to communicate with patients where the patients already are—online. Practices can keep it simple by only posting operating hours and the practice address, or go in-depth with patient stories and photos.

On the other hand, job seekers can use online networking to get an employer's attention. Another free business networking service called LinkedIn helps job hunters link to potential employers. This site gives them a snapshot of the potential employee's personality and credentials. He or she can create a good impression with a free, professional profile on this site. It is perfect for electronically getting your foot in the door before you even send out a résumé. And you may even find yourself being recruited without having to send a thing.

sustaining a positive work environment are a large part of the director's responsibilities. He or she reports to the CEO (Chief Executive Officer) and one career path is to advance to CEO or COO (Chief Operating Officer). At least five to 10 years in the insurance industry in claims, account management, or compliance. Directors of account management usually hold a bachelor's or master's in business or an accounting degree.

Director of Claims

The director of claims is a senior-level position that has direct responsibility for all claims operations. The director has full authority and responsibility for the strategic planning of all claims payment resources for an insurance company. This includes reviewing and evaluating all claims operations functions and assuring uniform and documented processes, engaging in short- and long-term planning, assuring quality in the claims process, preparing reports and budgets, and coordinating audits. The director supervises the claims team and works with senior executives, the IT department, sales staff, and account managers. He or she usually reports to the chief operating officer (COO). The career path can include a step-up to COO, CEO, or a vice-president position. Five to 10 years experience in insurance claims or another aspect of the insurance business is required. Claims directors usually have degrees in business or accounting.

Senior Health Care Analyst

This individual applies specialized technical and analytic skills to conduct data extraction, perform analysis, identify trends, and create reports utilizing various database, spreadsheet, and analytical tools. The analyst evaluates healthcare data and trends. He or she must be able to perform analytical and technical tasks that are based on an advanced understanding of managed care concepts, advanced methodological design, statistics, health care, and excellent writing. The analyst is charged with identifying potential questions from various data sources for further analysis and developing models to forecast the impact of possible recommendations. Analysts may report to the director of claims or to the director of account management. A minimum of five years of experience in analysis is necessary, and a master's degree in health care administration or a related field is preferred.

Medical Group Practices

A medical group practice is a formal association of three or more physicians and possibly other professionals such as dentists, optometrists, podiatrists, nurse practitioners, and physical therapists all engaged in providing health services. By a prearranged plan, the income generated from these practices are pooled and then redistributed to the members. Doctors benefit from group practice concepts because they save on overhead by pooling their expenses. Larger group practices require business managers or administrators who must be familiar with finances, patient accounts, handling records, and understanding personnel administration. There are several levels of opportunity for positions in administration in group practices.

Accounting Manager

Responsibilities for this job include assisting in determining financial objectives of the practice, analyzing and reporting accounting variances, and developing and monitoring accounting reports. In a large practice, this position would report to a chief financial officer. In a smaller practice, this position would likely be the senior accounting job. The manager supervises the activities of the accounting staff, which may include payroll, accounts payable, general ledger, tax payments, fixed assets, and purchasing activities. He or she also develops and implements accounting procedures appropriate for the practice, closes the monthly financial records according to accepted accounting practices, oversees operating budgets, and prepares for the annual independent audit of the practice. Knowledge of advanced accounting and how to manage an accounting system is necessary as is knowledge of reimbursement procedures. This person has to be skilled in budgeting, preparing financial reports, and computer spreadsheet applications. A bachelor's degree in accounting or finance is required, and a graduate degree in hospital administration is preferred.

Administrator

The administrator leads and directs operations in smaller practices and assists the CEO in those functions in larger group practices. He or she manages the daily operations of the practice by creating and implementing policies and procedures, supervises all staff, and develops strategic plans—or helps the CEO to do so—based on the identified needs of the patients. Essential knowledge includes principles and practices of health care planning, familiarity of policies of other local health care systems in order to interact effectively, and understanding of the policies and procedures of the medical office. The administrator has to exercise a high degree of judgment, initiative, discretion, and decision-making skills to achieve organizational objectives. Because the administrator is effectively in charge of all the other employees—which in a large practice may include several finance people, marketing staff, operational staff, information technology people, and others at several levels—he or she needs to be skilled in establishing and maintaining effective working relationships. The administrator may hold the title of vice-president and has to be able to communicate with physicians, patients, and administrative staff; construct and deliver reports to shareholders and boards; and be adept at financial and operational tasks. Many aspiring practice administrators start out as assistant administrators, operations managers, or as specialists in areas such as accounting or marketing. Usually, by the time an individual has reached this level he or she has had at least seven years of experience in health administration jobs in other group practices or health care settings. Minimum educational requirements include a graduate degree in health care administration or business administration or a combined degree such as finance and health administration, MBA and health administration, law and health administration.

Business Office Manager

Every group practice needs one. This person coordinates the activities of the practice as a business in order to maximize cash flow while improving patient, physician, and other customer relations. The manager plans and directs patient insurance, billing and collections, and data collection; manages the business office within an established budget; maintains contact with medical records and other departments to analyze patient records for billing purposes; and develops and oversees business systems and works with information technology to provide accurate billing and patient information. The manager should have knowledge of basic accounting and business management principles and knowledge of regulatory and insurance requirements. A degree in business or health management is preferred.

On the Cutting

Edge

Medical Coding

Cynthia Robinson, a health care practice consultant with Davenport, Marvin, Joyce & Co., LLP, in Greensboro, North Carolina, states that when she reviews the coding systems in the many practices where she consults, she uses the information as an educational tool to teach physicians and other office staff of the importance of the coding procedure. Medical coding is essentially the assignment of one number to every disease or condition and another number assigned to the procedure used to treat and diagnose the disease or ailment. It is applied to the patient's chart by experienced coders, some of whom are certified professional coders (CPCs). Codes are used to standardize the information for billing and for submitting information to insurance companies. In 2013, an international standardization of codes known as ICD-10 will be enforced. The 13,500 codes used now will increase to 58,000 codes and will confer these benefits: more accurate payment for new procedures; fewer miscoded, rejected, and improperly reimbursed claims; better understanding of the value of new procedures and health care outcomes; and improved disease management.

Communications Specialist

The specialist is responsible for the practice's telecommunications system, including the telephone system, voicemail, and conference-calling arrangements. He or she may report to a chief technology officer. This specialist develops and maintains policies and procedures for the communications infrastructure of the practice, trains new hires on the system, and troubleshoots and fixes problems associated with the system. Knowledge of current trends in communications is necessary, and the specialist should have skills in project management and problem-solving. A bachelor's degree in information technology is required and a graduate degree in health administration is usually a precondition for moving to a higher position in the practice.

Facilities Manager

These managers are responsible for running the physical facilities of an office and attending to related services, such as housekeeping, security, heating, ventilation, and grounds maintenance. This person monitors the supply inventory and maintains relationships with vendors, coordinates maintenance and cleaning activities, assists with new building projects, and oversees building security. The manager should be familiar with clinic policies and procedures, including the standard operating procedures for clinic operation, facilities management, and engineering. He or she should also know the federal, state, and local building codes and safety practices concerning hazardous conditions and materials. Skill in managing contracts with subcontractors is a plus. College is preferred, but a high school diploma is sufficient background if the individual has relevant experience.

Human Resources Manager

Responsible for overseeing workers' compensation, employee safety, retirement programs, benefit programs, hiring, and other human resources matters. In a larger practice, the HR manager may report to a director of human resources and may supervise HR assistants. The manager advises the administrative and clinical staff on human resource issues; reviews and processes worker's compensation claims; performs safety inspections and addresses risk factors; oversees the practice's retirement savings plan and profit-sharing programs; and takes on other human resources duties as the practice requires. Knowledge is required of worker's compensation regulations, management practices, and government regulations concerning employment. A bachelor's degree in human resources or a related field is required with a graduate degree in hospital administration recommended. Usually, the manager has reached this position after at least three years' experience in human resources in the health care industry.

Managed Care Analyst

The analyst in a group practice is responsible for analyzing utilization data from health plans claims. This includes preparing reports on medical service contracts and utilization data, updating the patient database, preparing capitation payments and updating the rate schedule, submitting claim data, and calculating health plan discounts. Knowledge of clinic policies and procedures is required along with knowledge of managed care contracts and utilization. Experience in claims and customer service is helpful for this position. A bachelor's degree in health administration or business administration is preferred.

Medical Assistant

These individuals work under the supervision of physicians, and perform a broad range of administrative and clerical duties. Administrative duties may include scheduling and receiving patients, maintaining medical records, medical transcription, telephone calls and correspondence, and managing practice finances. Clinical duties may include infection control, performing first aid and CPR, taking patient histories and vital signs, preparing patients for procedures, and performing selected diagnostic tests. A high school diploma or equivalent is desired, and there are associate's degrees in medical assisting that are preferred. A CMA (Certified Medical Assistant) designation can be earned by graduating from an accredited medical assisting school and then passing an exam given by the Certifying Board of the American Association of Medical Assistants (AAMA). With demand from 200,000 physicians, there is and will continue to be unlimited opportunities in this sector.

Medical Billing and Coding Specialist

Coders are responsible for coordinating, verifying, distributing, and managing all billable services. They coordinate with clinical staff to get charge information for patients, code the information according to a standard set of numerical codes, produce and distribute the billing information, and maintain records. The medical coder also serves to help document frequency of diagnoses and utilization of particular services and procedures associated with those diagnoses. He or she may audit and re-file appeals of denied claims. The medical coder may enforce federal mandates that require providers to use specific coding and billing standards through chart audits. Coders (sometimes called billers) usually report to the accounting manager in the practice. Some college is preferred and training in coding procedures is required. Coders can receive a Certified Professional

Coder (CPC) designation, which enhances opportunities for advancing to supervisory or consultant positions.

Medical Secretary

Medical secretaries perform highly specialized work requiring knowledge of technical terminology and procedures. They transcribe dictation, prepare correspondence, and assist physicians or medical scientists with reports, speeches, articles, and conference proceedings. They also record simple medical histories, arrange for patients to be hospitalized, and order supplies. They need to be familiar with insurance rules, billing practices, and the group practice's medical procedures. Specialized training programs are available for those wishing to become medical secretaries, and professional certifications are becoming increasingly important. At minimum, a high school education is required with some courses in health, biology, and clerical skills. Salaries vary according to skill and experience.

Military and Long-Term Care

The U.S. Department of Veterans Affairs (VA) operates a network of hospitals and clinics throughout the country. Health care administration positions are filled by former active military and by civilians if there are no veterans available. Long-term care facilities primarily cater to the elderly and disabled and share many of the same occupations as hospitals and group medical practices. Here are some examples of jobs at these facilities.

Administrator in a Long-term Care Facility

The primary duty of the long-term care facility administrator is to direct the day-to-day functions of the facility in accordance with current federal, state, and local standards. He or she also must be well-versed in the guidelines and regulations that govern long-term care facilities to assure that the highest degree of quality care can be provided to residents at all times. The administrator is delegated the administrative authority, responsibility, and accountability necessary for carrying out his or her duties. A bachelor's degree is necessary; a degree in public health or business administration is preferred. In most states, the administrator must also complete course requirements and pass an examination in order to be licensed.

Director of Nursing Home Activities

This person develops and implements programs that stimulate residents' physical and mental well-being. In this job, attention to the wide range of capabilities and limitations of the resident population is an important factor in designing programs and activities that meet recreational, social, and cultural needs. Once this knowledge is acquired, the director can organize group activities like lectures, painting and cooking classes, games, reading, and group exercises. The activities director often works with other institutional professionals, such as social workers and therapists, in order to develop appropriate programs. A bachelor's degree is preferred with at least two years previous work in a geriatric facility or a background in social work, recreation, or occupational therapy. Some states require accreditation through the National Council for Therapeutic Recreation Certification.

VA Medical Records Administrators

Department of Veterans Affairs (VA) medical records administrators make certain that medical records meet statutory and regulatory requirements. Administrators carry out medical records administration program goals by performing work requiring specialized knowledge of the concepts, principles, and practices of medical records administration. The work requires the application of analytical methods to medical records system issues, reviews, and studies. The administrative aspects of the work require an understanding of statistics, data processing, budgeting, contracting, procurement, personnel and property management. Medical records administrators need to have the equivalent of one year of active practice in the health information management field. This includes knowledge of the content and uses of health records, computerized information systems, principles and practices of health information administration, and the ability to apply knowledge of anatomy, pathophysiology, and medical terminology to health information management functions. The position also might require the possession of an active credential from AHIMA as a Registered Health Information Administrator (RHIA) or Registered Health Information Technician (RHIT).

VA Research Coordinators

Department of Veterans Affairs (VA) research coordinators manage day-to-day research activities, conduct structured interviews to rate symptoms and side effects, and collect study data. They also maintain complex existing databases and data spreadsheet files, assist project investigators in grant construction for future research proposals, and prepare all reports and submissions for the local Institutional Review Board and Research and Development committees. Research coordinators screen and evaluate candidates for clinical studies and use objective rating techniques to identify potential candidates for participation in studies.

VA Social Science Specialist

These specialists work in an interdisciplinary team of clinical and clinical support staff delivering both inpatient and outpatient mental health care. They provide clinical assessment, case management, and therapeutic services to patients. Social science program specialists apply knowledge in the behavioral and social sciences to assess patient backgrounds regarding psychiatric disorders, alcohol dependence, and substance abuse. Specialized knowledge of how military service impacts these disorders is required. They manage cases and conduct in-depth, individual and group counseling and therapy.

Chapter 4

Tips for Success

Tim Rice, CEO of a major hospital system that employees nearly 7,500 people, remarks that management skills are transferable, but leadership qualities have to be developed and nurtured. Interpersonal and leadership qualities are critical at any level of health care management. In fact, you should master these skills in order to achieve success as a health care manager.

The accomplished administrator must be adaptable and flexible and be able to take on new administrative skills as the situation requires. He or she must also be an effective leader, able to withstand the shifting tides of how health care institutions should be run, and be up-to-speed on policy and regulatory requirements. Donald Snook, a leader in hospital management and marketing, said in his book that the successful administrator has to have the magic three attributes: technical, interpersonal, and conceptual skills.

Technical Skills

In *Managing Health Services Organizations and Systems*, Longest and Darr say medical technology is "the procedures, equipment, and processes by which medical services are delivered and is defined as 'any discrete and identifiable regiment or modality used to diagnose and treat illness, prevent disease, maintain patient well-being, or facilitate the provision of health services.'" They also assert that advances in technology are responsible for as much as 70 percent of the rises in health care costs over the last 50 years. This is a double-edged sword for the administrator. He or she has to keep up with the technology, manage it appropriately, and control costs all at the same time. The administrator needs to be up-to-date on the latest X-ray machines, devices, information systems, and medicines in order to be able to conduct negotiations that are favorable to the institution's budget with vendors and to realistically assess the requirements of the medical staff when they request such technology.

Administrators are often put into the position of deciding whether a particular technology fits the kind of facility they are managing. For example, physicians in a medical practice may want the latest brain-imaging equipment because patients are demanding it, and new imagers provide much better output. But the practice may have only a few neurologists, and their needs have to be balanced against those of the other specialists in the practice. The administrator has to weigh the requests for technology against volume of usage, third-party payer regulations, community pressure, and the financial capabilities of the practice. Additionally, administrators also have to know enough to be able to manage their information technology (IT) staff and see to it that they produce the best results.

In short, administrators have to understand, utilize, and manage current technology and technological innovations in order to keep their organizations competitive. New technology is being introduced almost daily, and the successful manager has to find ways to keep up and engage in judicious decision-making when selecting appropriate technology for their institutions. What is critical for today's health care manager is having the knowledge to ask the right questions and having the leadership skills to implement technological innovations.

Interpersonal Skills

The administrator is not just a cog in the wheel of the institution but at the center of a variety of functional tasks. He or she must be adept at interacting with various levels of institutional members including physicians, nurses, board members, accountants, facilities employees, patients, and visitors. Competencies in team interaction are essential as well as the ability to promote cooperation among the other members of management.

If good human relations skills are missing, administrators will find themselves spinning their wheels when trying to solve complex personnel and strategic problems. An administrator who tries to accomplish tasks through command-and-control tactics, for example, rather than through alliances, discussions, and negotiation, will alienate the board and lose the confidence of his staff—not a good result. Human relations skills, discretion, and good judgment are critical factors to be developed consistently in the administrator who sets the tone of cooperation for the entire staff. For help in these areas, administrators can seek out leadership courses and counseling. In all this seriousness, do not forget a sense of humor—it comes in handy. Seasoned administrators can attest to the value of a joke or two in defusing a tense situation.

As Carson Dye, a health care management and executive search consultant points out, "although many leading health care organizations find that improving relationships with their employees and patients is the key to excellence, most still focus on financial factors to measure their success." People skills are often overlooked as contributors to good results because they are hard to measure. Dye lists the following skills as particularly important to success for those in the health care environment:

Fast Facts

Wireless Technology

Hospitals are finding novel uses for wireless technology. In February 2009, WakeMed Cary in North Carolina went live with a patient and asset tracking system that uses radio frequency identification technology that reads coded tags on equipment—like IV pumps, stretchers, blood pressure monitors—and patient wristbands. Administrators find the technology easy to implement and non-disruptive to hospital routines, and they expect substantial cost savings from the more efficient tracking it provides.

→ *Be a good listener.* Really listen with your head and heart and get the essential meaning of what someone is saying to you. Body language can say a lot, and tone of voice, hesitancy, and facial expression can all convey concerns that you might well have to confront. It is much better to listen than to dominate a conversation or act reactively, and the rewards can return to you tenfold.

→ *Show respect.* Many employees complain that their bosses just do not understand what they do every day. They translate this behavior as not caring or lack of respect, and a perception of lack of respect can be toxic to the health care workplace where the well-being of so many is at stake. The best administrators have regard for others, listen to their ideas, and care about their welfare and interests.

➤ *Take time for people.* Effective health care managers pay close attention to which way the wind is blowing when it concerns the people around them. They communicate and pay attention to others by fostering a relaxed environment. They take the time to attend employee events like picnics, award programs, charitable events, and more. They know that losing touch with the routines and concerns that occupy most of the staff can be detrimental to the effort to create a satisfactory—even tranquil—workplace.

➤ *Manage perceptions.* Tell the truth, so that others' imaginations do not go awry. The health care manager may be called upon to make many decisions—some of them not popular—that sometimes require an explanation to a variety of stakeholders. The physicians may be irritated that you have not ordered those new surgical goggles yet because of financial constraints. Tell them exactly why they have not gotten them without blaming anyone. The public relations person may be itching to launch a grand publicity program for the institution that paints it in very rosy colors, but you have your doubts because of some serious facilities issues that need to be corrected. Tell her exactly why now is not the right time.

➤ *Recognize others.* Emphasize the skills and achievements of others—not your own. Ultimately you will be measured by the success of those on your team, so let them do what they do best and recognize them for it. You will benefit in the long run.

➤ *Manage emotions.* Losing control of emotions in the workplace is just not acceptable. It marks you as unprofessional, ineffective, helpless, and perhaps feared. You might confront situations in which you are tempted to vent anger or annoyance. Restrain the impulse and look for a positive way to handle the situation. Health care managers are in settings where there are patients who are vulnerable to begin with, and they do not need to be exposed to unchecked emotions.

➡ *Focus on the needs of subordinates.* This is one of the most basic ways of maintaining interpersonal connections. Well-cared for subordinates whose values and needs have been recognized will respond in kind.

➡ *Display compassion.* Health care managers are often in situations where they are part of the clinical staff's decision-making in life-and-death situations. Working around health care institutions, health care managers often see patients who are grief-stricken, staff members who are dealing with sometimes unbearable patient situations, and personal issues that can affect performance. Show that you understand their suffering and do your best to provide a supportive environment.

➡ *Do not put others down.* Your stock does not rise if someone else's goes down. In fact, angry outbursts can have the opposite effect: Others will not respect you and they will not want you to lead them. Successful health care managers do not feel the need to disparage or belittle others.

➡ *Exhibit optimism.* It is easy to be negative when there is sickness and death around you, but health care administrators in such settings learn to overcome their despair with a sense of optimism. After all, optimism can be the pathway to less sickness and despair if it leads to action-oriented activities that help prevent illness. Optimism encourages projects that appear doomed from the start and can help you to rally support against seemingly insurmountable odds.

➡ *Be sensitive to those around you in times of disruption.* With downsizing, cut budgets, displacement, and major reorganizations, some areas of the health care industry are in crisis. And it looks like it will be in a state of flux for years to come, with a potential major overhaul of the U.S. health system. Your subordinates, your superiors, and the patients you serve are feeling it all. But if you can maintain sensitivity to others' reactions and perhaps serve as a sounding board, you can help maintain an even keel in the face of chaos.

Conceptual Skills

Conceptual skills concern the big picture and the broad perspective—the ability to see the forest for the trees. Effective administrators are able to keep the larger mission for the institution in mind while putting out the smaller fires on a daily basis. Administrators should pose the questions of how the institution fits into the community and what its contribution is to the local economy. They should also be mindful of what the political, social, and economic forces are that affect the institution. Being aware of these issues helps the administrator understand the broader health issues afoot in the community and to develop ways to deal with them. In order to do that, they must grasp a vision for going forward—a process that requires some degree of reflection and study. Some administrators, especially in larger health systems, are also considered community leaders, which can widen the scope of their responsibilities to the public. There are some specific attributes that contribute to good conceptual skills—good judgment, foresight, intuition, creativity, effective planning, problem-solving, and coordination of organization functions.

Leadership Skills

In such a rapidly changing field, not only technologically but also in terms of the regulatory environment, the health care administrator is the person who is often asked to develop the vision for the institution. Knowing when and how to deploy leadership skills is a great asset. Such leadership skills in today's health care organization include risk-taking, imagination, and a willingness to trust and engender trust.

Also important is the ability to work with and motivate teams. The work that health care administrators do with clinical teams, administrative teams, labor unions, community groups, and other groups of people is often evaluated in terms of how successful the administrator is in applying leadership principles. Knowing how and when to delegate is another measure of leadership competency, a skill that health care administrators—especially in large hospital systems—soon learn if they have not already mastered it.

There is a deficit of people who can serve as true leaders in the health care field. One reason is that new technology and new disbursement systems have added new headaches for health care managers. Reimbursement changes of the 1980s coupled with the mergers and acquisitions of the 1990s have significantly changed what health care managers do. Carson Dye says that "Re-engineering has displaced employees and deprived them of jobs and job security, lowered their morale, and eroded their trust. Physician-hospital integrations have threatened physician autonomy and leadership and caused organizational conflicts. Integrated health care systems have become cumbersome to manage[.]" In the midst of this seeming chaos, health care managers are trying to lead by just barely keeping their heads above water.

So, what are the leadership abilities that can be effective in complicated times and in complex institutions? Having the correct leadership values is the key to effective leadership for health care managers; that is, a value-based set of leadership imperatives is particularly suited to those who work in health care environments. Dye defines values as guiding principles that direct our behavior and our thoughts, and are formed early in life. What follows are the essential values-based leadership principles:

Respect

This is the value that encourages people to deliver consistently excellent performance. Respect is the opposite of the command-and-control model, where orders are given from powerful perches and the recipients are compelled to obey. A respectful leader—whether a hospital CEO, a medical billing supervisor, or a long-term care facility administrator—restrains his or her ego, admits mistakes, cares for and honors others, keeps an open mind, gives credit where it is due, and does not hesitate to ask for help. The respectful leader gathers trust.

Integrity

Why is it that leaders tend to think of themselves as having integrity but do not see much of it in their fellow leaders? Because it is hard to apply one's own moral compass to someone else, and decisions and actions that are seen as ethical in one situation may not seem so in the next. Nonetheless, integrity and ethics in leaders are especially critical to the health care administrator because the well-being of

Keeping in Touch

Making Connections

When you are in a position to talk with someone who can help you in your career—in the elevator, at a party, in the cafeteria where you work now, or at a university—what should you say? Simply tell the truth. Keep it simple and straightforward. Say you are looking for a job. Describe what you do in ten seconds and why it matters in ten seconds. Ask their advice and brainstorm with them about who else you can talk to. Then, be quiet and let them talk. You are interested in their opinion, so it is in your interest to keep the conversation going. Ask for specific names of people to contact. When the interaction is over, be extremely grateful.

the person receiving health services is at stake. Ethical decisions are risky because they are observed more closely and often necessitate that leaders reveal private opinions.

Servant Leadership

As an industry that serves the public, health care leaders are in effect "servants" to the needs of the organization and its constituents. A servant leader is someone who focuses on the mission of the organization, does not engage in selfish behavior, sincerely respects all people, recognizes the contributions of others, and helps followers to improve their skills and become better in their jobs so they can serve the organization better. Servant leaders look outward to the needs of the community and devote time and resources for its improvement.

Commitment

How dedicated do you think you will be to the health care profession? You can find that out easily by measuring your level of commitment to it. Like an athletic event, either you are in it or you are not. In fact, one health care professional expresses commitment as "getting the job done. You face all the hurdles and finish the race." To committed leaders, work is not a burden; it is a place where they find satisfaction and even joy when that right level of dedication is found.

Emotional Intelligence

Daniel Goleman (1998), who popularized the term *emotional intelligence*, said, "Emotional competence is particularly central to leadership." What exactly is emotional intelligence? Goleman would say that EI indicates a kind of intelligence or skill that involves the ability to perceive, assess, and positively influence one's own and other people's emotions. However, this does not mean that health care leaders or any leaders actually lack emotion. The trick is to find the right level that people can respond to and ultimately follow with confidence. Self-awareness is key to developing this skill.

Teamwork

Without effective teamwork, whatever setting your health care job is in, your efforts will probably be unsuccessful. Cooperation is especially important in the health care administration area because decisions cannot wait around forever—there are too many sick people depending on you. So park your ego at the door and build or participate in the teams that can reach your managerial and organizational goals. Many work-life activities are done better in teams.

Be Prepared for Change

Anyone who works in health care administration knows that change is the one constant, especially when dealing with technology. New devices, systems, policies on use, and organizational imperatives are occurring every day and can be the bane of the administrator's work life. Couple that with the rising costs of everything, and you have an ongoing and major headache that is not easily remedied.

For instance, a senior financial administrator may be asked his opinion on buying an updated CAT scan machine for the hospital. He is well aware that the current CAT scan machine does not have the latest bells and whistles, and the hospital he is employed by is losing patient days (the total number of inpatient days of care given in a specified time period) because they have not kept up with the two other hospitals in town that have newer technologies. However, he also knows that the budget is in the red. What does he do?

An IT professional at a military hospital is asked to assess the current information system's efficacy in supporting the hospital's medical records system. She knows that there are new programs being created for records systems that can vastly improve the current way of doing things, but she is also painfully aware that there are hierarchical obstructions peculiar to the military that can make implementing new technology very difficult if not impossible. What does she do?

Or the organization will completely alter its delivery system, the human resources department will change their criteria for hiring staff, the community will demand that care is more accessible, your supervisor will insist that its your job to thoroughly overhaul the IT system, the working schedule will go from five days to four because of budgetary restraints, there will be shortages of technical staff or nurses or physicians and you will have to hire from overseas, the building that houses your institution needs to be completely reconstructed according to latest guidelines. All of these can happen and much more.

Take heart. If you can keep some simple mantras in mind when confronting change, you will have a better chance at making the right decision. Nancy Lorenzi and Robert Riley, experts in biomedical informatics, suggest that the following areas need to be considered when thinking about a major change.

Make Proactive Versus Reactive Change

In the changing health care environment, one way for decision-makers in institutions to be proactive is to identify key or core values and focus their efforts around them. Administrators, public relations and marketing personnel, human resources staff, medical records supervisors, and others should be able to identify what is important to them in their environment. These are such things as teamwork, empowerment, innovation, quality, risk taking, cost consciousness, and other values. Find your organization's list of values and prioritize them when making a tough decision. This will help in making offensive change rather than defensive change.

Understand the Critical Global and Local Issues

You do not work in a bubble. Trends and activities are going on all around you that can affect your decisions. Understand your organization's local environment. Do you know whether the organization is open or hierarchical, what kinds of behaviors garner rewards, what the power structure is, and so on? If not, find out through surveys, talking to people, or just plain observation. Consult organizations that monitor global trends such as the Program on Information Resources Policy at Harvard University, and talk to key people. Being aware that the broad context, on both a local and global level, provides a more reliable benchmark on which to base a decision.

Keep Up with New Information

A simple fact is that if you want to go on the offensive with change, you have to keep up. The advances in technology, management, medical breakthroughs, legislation, and regulation make it necessary for the ambitious manager to stay ahead of the curve. Many of the professional organizations provide slates of educational offerings that include e-learning, Webinars, conferences, online courses, and much more. Look on any of the Web sites for the organizations listed in the "Resources" section, and you will likely find a tab titled "Education." The most successful managers make it a point to avail themselves of the many ways that they can stay informed in a rapidly changing environment.

Create a Vision for Change

Whether you are running a nursing home, are a medical coder, a CEO of a large hospital system, or a researcher at a school of public health, you need a vision. The vision can be a concept that you have worked out for yourself as to the best way that your job can contribute to the institution. For example, an administrator might dream of acquiring the best equipment and tools available. Or, a systems person might have strong ideas about providing the highest quality surgical reports. Whatever the vision, it serves to focus energies on the needs of the institution or setting and provides a place to start for the actions needed to fulfill it.

Identify the Key Issues for Leaders Who Confront Change

The person charged with making technological change must understand his or her role as the point person in the process of change. People can be happy or not with their decisions. When new technology is being installed, such as a new information system, and staff are not trained or willing to adjust to it, the point person takes the heat. Also, the person who leads change must be knowledgeable and committed. Without this, the leader may have trouble seeing a difficult change through. Next, the change leader should have both formal and informal power. A CEO, CIO, or CFO may have the organizational clout to push a change through, but if they do not have the respect and confidence of their subordinates the change will be difficult—if not impossible—to achieve. Last, the leader who effects change should be able to multitask. Can they easily shift among the technical, human, and conceptual areas when working up a plan that requires change?

Know These Things: Words from the Wise

Advice from those who have been through the health care management "wars" can be invaluable and can help you avoid some of the missteps that others have made before you. Anthony Kovner, a professor of management, and Alan Channing, a hospital CEO, have compiled a list of common problems that experience and inexperienced managers sometimes create for themselves. These concrete suggestions are terrific for the novice manager and the seasoned executive alike.

Learn How to Disagree

When "we've always done it this way" is being held up as the norm, but there is strong evidence that this particular way is not working in the current environment, think about these things before you go changing it. First, consider why the process or procedure was done that way in the first place, who benefits from it, and what will happen to whom if things change according to the way you see it. Second, beware of dividing up people into factions—those who agree and those who do not. Third, present those whom you seek to influence with the problem or challenge a challenge of their

Best Practice

Customizing the Cover Letter

If you want to get noticed, make sure you customize your cover letter for the particular job for which you are applying. Kenneth Hertz, an executive recruiter says, "During a recent search for a private-practice administrator, I received a cover letter outlining a candidate's experience in hospital administration, long-term care facilities, and developing his private consulting business. Not a word about his experience in private practices, or a link from his previous experience to private practice. Do you think this candidate made it to the next level?" (MGMA.org) Do not throw up obstacles by making it hard for the recruiter or employer to see the specific experience that is directly relevant to the job.

own. Ask them to solve it, and then tell them what is right about their solution.

Do Your Homework, and Do Not Worry So Much about Opposition

When you have what you think is a groundbreaking idea and someone asks you how it is going to work—be totally prepared to answer. Know how it might work under different circumstances and contexts and what might go wrong with it. Be sure that the idea fits the needs of your organization. If you have done your homework, people will at least realize that you have done your job. If you have not, then you will be perceived as wasting people's time.

Periodically Scan Your Job Environment

Is this you? Are you just slogging into work every day being held up by the momentum of your everyday tasks and giving no thought to what they mean to the organization? If so, you should be asking yourself some questions like: "Can the work you do be shared among other managers?"; "What is most important about your job?"; "Do you spend too much, just enough, or not enough time on the most important functions?"; "Have you influenced the organization in a major way lately?" This inventory-taking exercise can help you clear out things that are getting in your way so you can concentrate on what is important, and it can strengthen the focus on the true values that are inherent in your job.

If You Cannot Do What You Want, Do What You Can Do

There are going to be times when you think a decision is good for the institution, but the trustees, the physicians, the clinical staff, and others may not see it as timely or in their interest. Do not make it "my way or the highway"—just keep working hard, and the idea's time may come. In the meantime, you can build and sustain your authority as a voice for good decision-making by getting results on other projects and staying focused on what is good for the institution.

No Gossiping

It is not high school, and it is obviously not professional to talk about someone who is not present—at least in personal terms. No gossiping about someone's marital adventures, family problems, or personal quirks. This will just gain you a reputation as unprofessional. What you really want to know about people is how they feel about important issues that relate to the running of and the well-being of the organization, and your questions about them should be restricted to those issues.

About Leaving Your Job

The reasons usually given for leaving a job in health care management are: advancement is blocked, the wish to try something new, dissatisfaction with a boss, or a boss's dissatisfaction with you. Whatever the reason, when the idea first starts forming in your head to leave, it will probably be long before you are ready to do so. During this time, you should be growing your network of people who can help you hone in on the opportunities that you are now ready for and who can also guide and give advice. You should also be still getting results on your present job since you will want to leave with a good recommendation.

What to Do When People Attack You

When this happens, the person who is attacking you is usually reacting emotionally to something you have said or done. When things cool down, try to find out what that is. There may a general feeling of dislike and fear of you from certain people, or perhaps you are not seen as one of them because of your age, race, ethnic group, or other factor. You may be perceived as arrogant, playing favorites unfairly, inconsiderate, or bullying. If any of these things are even half-true, then you need to work on yourself. However, learn to discern when people are attacking your person because of your policies. You have a right to stand up for your policies but not a right to act badly. Know the difference.

Do Not Expect from Others What You Do Not Do Yourself

You know that there are certain things you would not do yourself, so why ask them of others? Also, acknowledge that subordinates and peers will not do things in the same way. The important thing to do is to show that you are committed to whatever task that you and your group are engaged in, and to demonstrate that you not only have high expectations of your subordinates but also of yourself. This says to them that you will dig in your heels when needed and will not stand aside just waiting for results.

Preparing to Be a Health Care Administrator

There are many paths leading to a career in this field. A music major turned pharmacist, who later got a graduate degree in health care administration, became the head of a large hospital system. A nurse who spent 15 years in clinical care became interested in the policy side of health care and went back to school for a degree in public health. Some start out with the idea that health care administration is the route they want to pursue, but because of the relative lack of understanding of what health care managers do, many more take a rather circuitous path to being an administrator. Here is some advice on making that path shorter and smoother.

INTERVIEW

The Essentials of Getting Ahead

Joel C. Mills
CEO, Advanced Health Care, High Point, North Carolina

What does it take to do a good job in this field?
There are several things:

(1) It is very important to learn it from the ground up. I started out as delivery driver, worked in a billing capacity, and came to understand the nuts and bolts of what made the business run. It allowed me to understand the roles and the organization and to graduate to more strategic functions and thinking. If you know the basic building blocks, you can take those things and become a better leader and strategic thinker.

(2) Understand the balance between patient care and the business side. If you get out of whack with that, you will not be successful in health care administration because the people you are leading—if they are in the patient-care setting—are all on the caring side. If I came across as completely money-oriented, I would not be successful in this setting where we take care of 20,000 patients every day.

(3) Have value-based reasons for being in the health care administration industry. It is a great industry to be in for helping people, and it is also a growth-oriented business and will be here for the long-term. Because we are not-for-profit, we have a more value-centered approach and a greater purpose. If you go into it and do not have some of that caring side—that feeling that you can do something for patients and for the community—eventually you will be found out and will not be successful.

(4) Be your own personal advocate. Nobody is going to look out for you but you. Make yourself available to people you can ask questions of. Search out mentors. Many of the professional organizations that serve health care administrators have mentoring programs. The mentor likes to be sought out, and it is a good opportunity for the mentee. I see people waiting around to be chosen instead of being proactive in their own career development.

(5) Education is important. In many health care settings, there are certain requirements for particular jobs. There are graduate-level degrees that are necessary for certain positions. You do not neces-

sarily get jobs because of your education, but you can be excluded from jobs by not having the right education.

(6) Acquire good communication skills. Being able to speak in public and deal with groups at all levels can be a separator for people. There are some who learn the business and grow and develop, but they are not able to get in front of people and convey their thoughts. Sometimes that holds them back.

(7) Understand the finances of the institution. You need to understand the numbers, or you will run into a glass ceiling if you cannot comprehend budgeting and numbers. You need to understand the difference between an income statement, a balance sheet, a capital budget, and those types of things. You need to have a good working knowledge of those things.

(8) Interpersonal skills are critical. You need to know how to make connections with people. Such things as relationship-building, accessibility, making yourself somebody who is thought of positively are important. You need to give more than you take in every interaction you have. If you are not giving back, it will eventually hurt you.

What do you think contributes to failure?

(1) Failure to grow. People become stagnant, and are not willing to work on themselves. They get to a point where they are not successful. They may lose the support of others, especially if the organization itself is growing.

(2) People who are dictatorial. Some people are very regimented, which can hurt them. If you are not flexible and are not able to accept input, you will not be successful.

What specific advice do you have for planning a career in health care administration?

(1) Be willing to start at the ground floor—whether that be at a patient-care level, customer service level, billing clerk. Learn the details of what is happening in that business, and once you have mastered that look for opportunities to progress.

(2) Be a generalist and not a specialist. Look for opportunities in other parts of the business. If you are in the billing area and you are interested in a sales position, you can use some of the skills you learned on the billing side of the business in the sales side.

(3) Have a personal and professional development plan. Develop a network, choose mentors, and express a specific desire to work up development plans. You should have a personal plan that includes

(continues on next page)

INTERVIEW

The Essentials of Getting Ahead (continued)

all phases of your life outside of work and a professional development plan that would include the goals you want to reach. The professional plan should include such things as education needed, skill sets you want to develop, conferences and seminars you want to attend, areas of yourself you want to improve through 360-degree feedback [provided 'all around' by supervisors, peers, and subordinates] and other methods.

What advice do you have for job-hunting and interviewing?
The best advice I have is to network with someone who can make introductions. A personal recommendation is very valuable. You certainly have to stand on your own and have a good interview—have your research done on the organization, know what the job is about, and be specific about what you can do.

When I look at résumés, I look for education and experience. I also look for someone who has not been a job-hopper and has shown loyalty to an organization. Commitment and stability are important.

At interviews, you have to be yourself. Believe in what you are saying. If you are just there to put on a marketing show, it will not work. If you believe in what you are doing, it makes the best impression. We do not try to fit people into a box. We try to construct a box around the right person. So, we look for the best people who we can develop.

We look for people who are flexible and who can develop relationships. For instance, when hiring for our sales team we look for likable people who can work well with potential clients and who are committed to the organization and are self-mtotivated. For marketing people, we want people who know how to dig out the appropriate data and are organized.

Planning Your Career Path

You have already gotten your feet wet in the field. Maybe you are a marketing assistant in a long-term care facility, an assistant to the senior administrator in a large, urban hospital, or a member of the finance team at an ambulatory care center. You have enjoyed the work, learned a lot, and want to get more serious about delving deeper into health care management—even though you may have started as a general marketing person or an accountant with little knowledge of the health care field in general. You want to go higher and maybe wider. Where do you go from here?

Three well-traveled paths for those already in the field are to improve the situation where you are, search for a job in other institutions, or get a degree. If you want to stay put, you can ask for more money, more responsibility, and/or a promotion. This can be done in stages. For instance, the marketing person can ask to develop some projects on her own instead of assisting others, and then ask for a promotion when having proved herself. If you are in a large hospital system, the employment opportunities are numerous and you can move more easily in large departments or from one facility to another.

If you want to work elsewhere because you feel that you have learned and given all that you can to your current job, the question is when to move. You might not want to make a switch immediately. You may also have personal reasons for not making the move just yet. But if the ultimate goal is to move on and push your career forward, consider these factors recommended by Anthony Kovner and Alan Channing:

→ *Location*. If you are more flexible, you will be more likely to find a job. Also, in areas where health services organizations are expanding there are likely to be more jobs.

→ *Hours*. Hospital administrators typically work long hours. Ambulatory care managers or compliance officers tend to work more regular hours. Your personal situation, preferences, and level of ambition come into play when considering this factor.

→ *Type of organization*. You may prefer a nonprofit hospital, which is often large and has a variety of positions; a public facility where you can exercise your altruistic leanings; or a for-profit job like health care consultant or insurance analyst where your specialized skills come into play.

→ *Boss*. The more you know about who you will be working for, the better. As an already experienced worker, you may have experienced a bit of the good, the bad, and the ugly when it comes to bosses. The goal is to work with someone under whom you can fulfill your career goals.

➡ *Risk.* How much risk can you tolerate in order to reap the rewards that might result? Ask this question when considering that next move forward.

➡ *A good fit.* Know thyself. Self-knowledge will help you figure out whether you can adapt to a new set of responsibilities that will stretch you. If you are not aware of personal strengths and weaknesses, moving up could turn into a bad career choice.

Degree Options

Degrees in health care management are available at baccalaureate, master's, and doctoral level. Most baccalaureate programs offer three options: general management, specialist training in a specific discipline such as financial management, or a focus on a specific segment of the industry such as ambulatory care. Many students who complete undergraduate degrees in health administration will go on to complete graduate degrees. Others enter health care administration careers in hospitals, long-term care facilities, physician practices, or other health services organizations.

At the master's level, a traditional route is a master's degree in health administration (MHA) or public health (MPH). However, there is also the option of a business degree with a concentration in health services management, a joint degree in business administration and public health, or in health care and law. AUPHA (Association of University Programs in Health Administration) claims that the following degree designations are held by their members: MBA, MHA, MHM, MHPA, MHS, MHSA, MHSc, MHSM, MPA, MPH, MS, MSc MSHA, MSHSA, MSHA, and MSPH (M=master's; 2nd M=management; B=business; H=health; A=administration; S=services or science; Sc=science; SM=services management; P=public; thus, MSHSA is master's of science in health services administration).

Graduate programs generally last two years and include courses in health care policy, organizational behavior, law, marketing, health care financing, human resources, leadership, and more. Programs may also include a supervised internship, and some health care facilities require a one-year residency for their new administrators. Some programs have a strong fieldwork or experiential component that combines academic coursework with applied work in health care organizations. Graduate programs can be fulltime, part-time, in the form of executive programs for working health care administrators, and even distance education.

Which Master's Degree is Best—MBA, MPH, MHA?

According to the American College of Health Care Executives (ACHE), if one has a bachelor's degree in business with a major in accounting or finance, odds are the value added by completing an MBA *without a health care concentration* will be marginal because it will be too general and not offer the targeted knowledge needed in the profession. For such people, attending an accredited MHA or MPH program may make more sense. The MBA-based health administration programs offer a concentration in health care. Some of these programs may have only recently become part of their universities' business schools after an earlier period when they were independent units or were in another academic setting. Accreditation is important in that it boosts your earning power and puts you in with the foremost professional networks in the industry. The relevant accreditation to look for in graduate programs in health care is from the Commission on Accreditation of Health Care Management Education (CAHME). CAHME accredits master's level programs that offer MBAs, MHAs, MPAs, MPHs, and other degrees such as MHSAs (Master of Health Services Administration).

A common set of characteristics can help distinguish among programs offering a master's in health administration whether the degree is a MBA, MPH, or a MHA. Even though you may be considering a half-dozen or more CAHME-accredited programs, you should try differentiating them by looking at the following: 1) who is on the faculty, 2) what they publish, 3) how much they serve or consult with health care organizations, and 4) whether there is a large and distinguished alumni body that supports the program by hiring students and graduates for internships and for fulltime jobs.

Finally, you may want to consider whether a program offers a joint-degree option such as an MHA/MBA or an MHA/JD. Although completing such programs may require longer time commitments and cost more, they will provide greater career flexibility in the long term.

Getting the Job You Want

You might think that looking for a job in the health care management field is like looking for a job in any other field. There are some similarities, but there are also some striking differences. Below is some advice on job hunting that will point you in the right direction.

Developing a Network

In health care administration, as in most fields, networking and personal contacts account for most job placements. Donald Snook's advice for developing an effective network is to draw up a network identification form by creating four headings—professional colleagues, academic associations, friends and acquaintances, and relatives. Be judicious about whom you use to fill in those columns. Does cousin Ryan, the owner of a heating and air-conditioning company, come in contact with many people in the health care management field? Probably not. But does Aunt June, who has worked in marketing for many years have some influence? Indeed, yes. She may know marketing people at the local long-term care center or hospital. Ask the people on your list to help you contact anyone they can think of who is associated with health care—hospital administrators, HR directors, public relations or marketing staff, housekeeping supervisors, facilities managers, and so forth.

Other Places to Search for Job Opportunities

How about the other 25 percent of jobs in the health care industry that are not secured through contacts? These jobs are obtained primarily through online job search sites, newspapers, and the job sites of professional organizations in the field. The online sites like Monster and Hot Jobs can give you a good idea of the opportunities available and where the jobs are. There are also health care-specific Internet job sites like http://www.HealthJobsUSA.com, http://www. health carejobbank.com, http://www.explorehealthcareers.org, and http://www.healthcaresource.com.

Also, check the professional organizations' Web sites listed in the "Resources" section of this book. Many of them also have job banks and career advice. For instance, the American College of Health Care Executives (ACHE) maintains an online job bank and other career services. Watch newspaper listings for jobs that range from the executive-level ones (*New York Times, Wall Street Journal*) to searching the local listings under group-practice administrator, medical assistant, hospital laundry supervisor, assistant administrator, marketing or public relations specialist in a hospital setting, health educator, health or patient advocate, and so forth. Look under the management and general sections in addition to the health care section. Some professional journals that contain job listings are: *Hospitals & Health Networks, Modern Health Care, Health Care Financial Management, American Journal of Public Health, The Clinical Supervisor,* and *Healthcare Executive Magazine.*

Your Résumé

The two most popular résumé styles used by candidates for health care administration jobs are the functional and accomplishment résumés, according to Snook (2007). Although they both contain general autobiographical data, they differ in their approach to employment descriptions. The functional type lists the actual jobs with minimal information about accomplishments in the job. For example,

2000–04
ABC Long-term Care Facility, Anytown, USA
Assistant administrator in a 75-bed facility.
Reported to senior administrator.
Supervised five people and was responsible for a budget of
$500,000.00.

The accomplishment résumé, on the other hand, emphasizes specific successes. So the above entry might look like this:

2000–04
Assistant Administrator
Oversaw the creation and production of a procedures manual
for employees of the facility. Came in under estimated budget
for the project.

The accomplishment résumé has a slight edge over the functional one in that it shows prospective employers what you are capable of in the future. Here are some "Dos" and "Do Nots" for developing a good résumé:

Do start a permanent résumé file; list all your education, experience, and achievements; know the kind of work you are seeking; be specific—give examples of projects that you have done; be quantitative—provide numbers of major reports written, problem situations, and so forth; use action words like *allocate, debate,* and *propose*; keep it to one or two pages; and be sure to check for misspellings and typos.

Do not include job requirements; discuss lack of employment or reasons for leaving your current job; use visual or verbal gimmicks (i.e., clip art); criticize former employers; include a photograph of yourself; overuse the word "I"; or use abbreviations.

The Cover Letter

Your cover letter should facilitate the process of choosing your résumé out of a slush pile that likely is sitting on the hiring person's desk. If you feel you cannot write an effective one, consult the many books on the subject or search Web sites like About.com that has a section on cover letters.

Cover letters can open the door or slam it in your face—so consider them carefully. First, make sure that your name, complete address, home and cell phone numbers with area codes, and the date are on the top of the letter. Include your business phone as well. Make it easy for the employer to contact you. Next, if responding to an ad, try to address the person by name if available. You might have to call the hospital or consult your network to get the name.

In the body of your cover letter, first establish why you are writing. For instance, "I am writing because I have been referred to you by Jane Doe regarding an accounting position in your hospital," or "I am writing you in response to your advertisement for a medical assistant that appeared in *The Daily Bugle* on June 4." Go on to very briefly emphasize the particular areas of expertise that you possess that apply to the position. For instance, if you are a finance person talk about how you developed a unique system, how you saved money for the place you work now, how you trained assistants to do more responsible jobs. Say just enough to get the reader to want to consult your résumé and then sign off. An effective letter is short and a to-the-point. Employers do not want to read on and on about you.

The Interview

You are probably familiar with interviewing from your past job experience. The interviewer will ask a few polite questions to break the ice and then some questions specific to the job you are applying for, such as: What do you know about our hospital or institution? What do you consider your strongest management skill? Why do you want to join our staff? How do you think your education and past experience have prepared you for this job? What will you be doing in five years? Ten years? What else can you tell me about yourself?

Interviewing can be a sweat-inducing experience, but there are some things you can do to make your interview a more successful one: Practice beforehand; be yourself; tell the interviewers what you can do for them; be prepared to discuss your strongest assets; do not end on a negative; do not waste time discussing your hobbies or personal life; be specific, to the point, and keep to the facts; never argue with the interviewer; and be a good listener.

Also, be sure to emphasize the professional organizations that you belong to if you have gone that far in your career in health administration. You might find that you have a built-in ally in the interviewer who may also belong to MGMA, AHIMA, or ACHE, for example. Do not forget to do your homework about the hospital, including key people and events in the news, so that you will be prepared for a general conversation about the institution. Follow up the interview with a thank-you note, and add anything important that you feel you might have omitted.

Chapter 5

Talk Like a Pro

You are going to need to know what you are talking about on a job interview, on the job itself, and at conferences and meetings. This chapter is meant to help you acquire the lingo of the business. The first section runs through a series of key terms that cover just about any area of management, activity, regulation, law, or facility you are likely to come in contact with.

ability to pay   Criterion used to determine the source of payment in which the provider of care or a third party like an insurance company identifies available resources of patient or family.

academic medical center   Medical complex consisting of a medical school, university, and teaching hospitals.

accountability   The requirement of an individual to be responsible for actions taken and to be answerable to the consequences of those actions.

accreditation of health care facilities   The process by which an organization recognizes a provider, a program of study, or an institution as meeting predetermined standards. Two organizations that accredit managed care plans are the National Committee for Quality Assurance (NCQA) and the Joint Commission on Accreditation of Healthcare Organizations (JCAHO). JCAHO also accredits hospitals and clinics. CARF (Commission on Accreditation of Rehabilitation Facilities) accredits rehabilitation providers.

Problem
Solving

Capitation

Health care managers, especially in their roles as financial managers, need to be concerned about capitation, which calls for a flat rate to be paid no matter the procedure and can lead to a level of risk for the institution. The challenge for managers is to identify the risks, whether they are worth taking, and the best strategy for dealing with them.

Allen, a controller in a medium-sized hospital, was faced with an increasing number of heart transplants. Although the procedure still represented a small percentage of the overall surgeries performed at his institution, the operations were very expensive and represented a risk to the institution because they would receive payments for them that did not cover costs. Allen had to find a way to reduce the risk. He considered purchasing stop-loss insurance, which covered large claims. But the hospital's insurance plan was a new one, and the stop-loss option was not available for new plans. After attending a specific session on reducing risk at a professional conference, Allen became familiar with another option—the risk band. Allen was a bit hesitant at first, because the risk band involves some flexibility in the capitation rate and it would probably decrease profit. The risk band adjusts the capitation rate when utilization is higher (or lower) than expected. Allen was not sure he wanted to deal with a moving target, when a fixed capitation rate was easier on the existing systems in terms of documentation. So, he looked at another option—carving out services. This is where he could send his risky cases to another provider in the network so that the capitation rate no longer applied—for instance, sending the cardiac patients to a facility in another city. That felt to Allen like abandoning his responsibility to the patients in his community, and he soon rejected this option. Allen talked to Stanley, a CEO of a hospital system in another state, who had some success with risk bands. Then he further used his network by talking with and e-mailing other colleagues who had experience with risk bands. Allen weighed the potential loss of profit against the community needs for heart transplants, and decided for the risk band option.

accredited record technician   An individual who has been trained and practices in the field of medical records systems and procedures.

action analysis   The process that occurs when a manager examines the viability of a plan, predicts whether a decision is sound, and analyzes whether the courses of action are effective.

action research   The process of collecting data about an ongoing organizational system, feeding it back into the system, and then altering a variable within the system in response to this data.

active listening   Helping someone with whom you are speaking to say precisely what he or she really means through asking questions and probing for the most accurate expression.

activities director   A person responsible for developing and supervising activities provided to patients in a long-term care facility.

acute care hospital   A hospital with an average length of stay of less than 30 days.

adaptive organizations   Organizations that display a minimum of bureaucratic features and that have cultures that encourage worker empowerment and participation.

administration   The management and direction of the affairs of health care organizations and professional practices. The words "administration" and "management" are used interchangeably.

admission certification   A form of medical review involving an assessment of the medical need of admitting a patient to a hospital or other program or institution, usually for insurance and HMO purposes.

admissions professional   A health care professional other than a physician who is responsible for admitting a patient to a health facility. Often the first employee a patient sees, the admissions professional is responsible for facilitating the admissions process.

admitting diagnosis   Provided on admission to a hospital or other health care facility that explains the medical reason for admission and is used for coding purposes.

affiliated hospital   One that is affiliated with another health-related institution, such as a school of dentistry, medicine, nursing, and so forth.

affirmative action   Preference in hiring and promotion to women and minorities, including veterans, senior citizens, and people with disabilities.

allied health personnel Health workers other than physicians, dentists, podiatrists, and nurses. These are individuals who have technical training and/or licenses in such areas as nutrition, support occupations, technicians, aides, physician assistants, and so forth.

any-willing-provider (AWP) laws These laws allow any physician to have access to a health plan's enrollees at the negotiated price. In other words, an HMO or insurance company cannot restrict their access to patients if they meet the plan's guidelines. AWPs lessen price competition among physicians because they cannot be assured of having a greater number of enrollees and thus have no incentive to compete on price.

arbitration A form of dispute resolution that involves a neutral third party who acts as a judge and issues a binding decision.

asset management The ability to use resources efficiently and operate at minimum cost.

avoidance In conflict management, being uncooperative and unassertive.

balance billing When the patient is billed the difference between a third-party payer's approved fee and the physician's fee.

balanced scorecard A performance-management tool that measures whether small-scale activities of an organization are aligned with large-scale activities. It forces organizations to look at not just finances but at operations, marketing, and development in order to discern in which areas they can most successfully focus their efforts.

base compensation An employee's salary or hourly wage.

benchmarking Using external comparisons to evaluate an organization's current performance and identify possible future actions.

bottom-up change Initiatives for change come from people throughout an organization and are supported by the efforts of middle- and lower-level managers acting as change agents.

budget Financial plans that commit resources to activities, projects, or programs during a prescribed length of time, depending on the accounting system used by the institution.

bundling An insurance term that means the consolidation of two or more services like supplies, drugs, or other medical services in order to create fewer categories for ease of payment.

Everyone Knows

Communication Techniques

Health care is undergoing dramatic change. Jo Manion suggests these communication techniques for health care managers during times of change

- be available and accessible
- find multiple ways to describe a concept
- convey complex concepts simply
- repeat key messages at least seven to nine times
- share stories that communicate
- use metaphors that fit what you need to communicate
- avoid mixed messages
- be certain that your messages are received
- be aware that in times of high emotion during change, people are not as receptive to messages

bureaucracy   A form of organization based on logic, order, and the legitimate use of formal authority.

business strategy   Creating, implementing, and evaluating a set of imperatives that sets the direction that will enable an organization to achieve its long-term objectives.

cafeteria plans   Allows employees to choose from a "menu" of one or more qualified benefits for medical coverage like pretax insurance premium deductions, flexible spending accounts, and dependent care spending accounts.

capital budgeting   The process of selecting long-term assets—like new machinery, replacement machinery, new plants, new products, and research development projects— whose useful life is greater than one year.

capitation   A flat payment to a provider per person cared for. The provider assumes the risk that the payment will cover the cost of the patient's care.

career planning   Structured advice and discussion sessions to help individuals plan career paths and programs of personal development.

certificate of need   Prior approval from a state agency for capital expenditures exceeding certain predetermined levels.

chain of command   Line of authority that vertically links all positions with successively higher levels of management.

change leader   A person or group who takes leadership responsibility for changing the existing pattern of behavior of another person or social system.

change readiness index (CRI)   Scorecard system asks team members to rate their health care organization and specific teams or groups in categories such as patient service, organizational reaction, and readiness to change.

COBRA (Consolidated Omnibus Budget Reconciliation Act)   COBRA provides certain former employees, retirees, spouses, former spouses, and dependent children the right to temporary continuation of health coverage at group rates. This coverage is only available when coverage is lost due to certain specific events such as termination, or, for dependents, the death of the covered employee. Length of coverage for employee and their dependents is 18 months for loss of job and 36 months for dependants in the event of the employee's death.

codes of ethics   Official written guidelines on how to behave in situations where ethical dilemmas are likely to occur.

cohesiveness   The degree to which members are motivated to remain part of a team.

collaboration   In conflict management, being both cooperative and assertive; problem-solving.

collective bargaining   The process of negotiating, administering, and interpreting labor contracts that involves union member and company management,

communication   An interpersonal process of sending and receiving symbols with messages attached to them.

comparable worth   The notion that persons performing jobs of similar importance should be paid at comparable levels.

competitive advantage   An attribute or combination of attributes that allows an organization to outperform its rivals.

compressed workweek   Any work schedule that allows a fulltime job to be completed in less than the standard five days of eight-hour shifts.

conceptual skill　The ability to think analytically and solve complex problems.

confrontation meeting　Intensive, structured meetings to gather data on workplace problems and plan for constructive actions.

constructive stress　Stress that acts in positive ways—energizing and performance- enhancing—for the individual and organization.

consultative decision　Decision made by a leader after asking group members for information, advice, or opinions.

contingency leadership theory　Leadership theory in which a leader's success depends on a match between leadership style and situational demands.

contingency planning　The process of identifying a series of alternative plans for achieving an objective. Various alternative plans may be implemented according to future events, opportunities, or barriers.

continuity of care　Uninterrupted care provided from the initial contact with a physician or clinic through all instances of a patient's medical needs.

continuous business development (CBD)　A building-block approach to all departmental activities in management efforts. Every effort undertaken by the department should be done to make it a stronger, more progressive entity than it was prior to the effort.

continuous quality improvement (CQI)　An organizational process in which employee teams identify and address problems in their work processes, intended to create a continuous flow of process improvements in patient care.

contract services　Services purchased from individuals and organizations that are not on staff or the regular payroll of a health care facility.

control group　A group of persons who are similar to an experimental group but who are not subject to treatment in a research study. The control group is used for comparison.

convalescence care　Care furnished to restore an individual's ability to function at normal levels after an illness or injury.

coordination of benefits (COB)　The contract provision that prevents a claimant from profiting by collecting from two different group plans such that the total is greater than actual expenses.

copayment   A type of cost sharing in which insured persons or organizations pay a specific amount per health service rendered.

corporations of health care   Where hospitals restructure themselves into new corporate forms and become active in non-health related areas of business.

cost   In health care delivery, this is the total economic investment in the delivery of health care within the particular institutional environment.

cost containment   A group of strategies used to control the cost of health care services that can include cost-sharing approaches, benefit designs, provider contracts, and discount of set charges.

covered charge   A billed charge for an item, service, or procedure defined in a health insurance plan as a benefit.

credentialing   In health care management, a process whereby certification can be achieved through a variety of methods—writing papers, passing an exam, amassing experience and education. Certification demonstrates that the individual has taken extra steps to achieve a professional designation and show commitment to the field. Examples of certifications are the FACMPE (Fellow of the American College of Medical Practice Executives) and FACHE (Fellow of the American College of Healthcare Executives). Certification is also sometimes called board certified.

critical path method   A form of project management that identifies a project's critical path or sequential activities.

customary charge   A physician's median charge for a particular service for most of his or her patients.

data set   An aggregation of items of information that describe an element, episode, or aspect of health care, such as hospital admission.

day, inpatient bed count   The number of inpatient beds available for use in one 24-hour period.

decision tree   A graphic method of presenting various alternatives in a decision-making process. Risks, information needs, and courses of action for each alternative are visible in the form of a tree with branches.

deductible   This is the amount that an insured party must pay before the benefits of a health plan begin.

defensive medicine   When health care practitioners use excessive tests and measures for the purpose of avoiding a malpractice suit.

detail person   This is a salesperson from a pharmaceutical manufacturer who promotes prescription drugs for use by health care providers.

device   Equipment that is used in the recovery process that is not a drug, such as crutches, wheelchairs, and cardiac pacemakers.

diplomate status   Many physicians acquire diplomate status in their specialties, which means that they are board certified—like D-IM, which is Diplomate in Internal Medicine.

direct patient-care support services   Such services as housekeeping and chaplaincy services fall within this designation because they do not involve direct clinical application.

discharge coordinator   A person who arranges with health or community agencies to coordinate care for a discharged patient.

doctor-patient relationship   This describes the personal relationship and not the economic one. It can take the form of several models in which the relationship is characterized as a purely factual exchange of information, a paternalistic one where the physician takes an interest in the psychological well-being of the patient, or a contractual one wherein there is an exchange of information and decision-making.

economies of scale   The relationship between cost per unit and size of organization.

electronic medical record (EMR) systems   Through computerized information, EMR provides caregivers with immediate access to patient information through connectivity to the Internet, e-mail, and other real-time tools.

emotional intelligence (EI)   A term originated by Daniel Goleman that describes the ability to identify, assess, and manage one's own emotions and those of others. The concept puts forth the notion that self-awareness, self-regulation, motivation, empathy, and social skills are necessary to achieve effective emotional intelligence.

enterprise resource planning system (ERP)   An overarching system that coordinates and provides interoperability among all the computers and computer systems in an organization.

ERISA (Employment Retirement Income Security Act of 1974)   The basis of most employee benefit legislation. Even new laws and changes are normally designed as amendments to ERISA. This federal legislation allows for and sets guidelines regarding a group's ability to self-fund their benefits.

ethical choices   Situations in which a moral choice has to be made when taking an action. Considerations that contribute to the decision may be community standards, the individual's personal ethical framework, and the perception of right and wrong.

executive coaching   A formal engagement in which a qualified coach works with an organizational leader in a series of dynamic, confidential sessions designed to establish and achieve clear goals that will result in improved managerial performance.

Family Medical and Leave Act (FMLA)   Passed in 1993, FMLA permits employees to take up to 12 weeks of unpaid leave each year for family or medical reasons without the risk or fear of losing their jobs.

fee-for-service (FFS)   A method of payment for medical care services in which payment is made for each unit of service provided.

fixed costs   Costs that do not vary with output.

flexible spending account (FSA)   A benefit option that reimburses employees for certain expenses they incur. Money is deducted from paychecks on a pre-tax basis. It most often covers reimbursements for medical expenses not covered under other insurance, or reimbursements for child care expenses.

gatekeeper   In many HMOs, this is the primary care physician who is responsible for the administration of the patient's treatment and who coordinates all medical services.

glass-ceiling effect   First coined as a term that represents an invisible but transparent barrier preventing qualified women from reaching the top levels of management, it now applies to minorities and the disabled as well.

health care network   A variety of medical services that come together to provide comprehensive health care.

Health Insurance Portability and Accountability Act (HIPAA)   Passed in 2003, HIPAA protects employees from access to personal health information and limits employers' ability to use employee health information.

health maintenance organization (HMO)   A type of managed care plan that contracts directly with or directly employs participating health providers to offer a comprehensive plan to the consumer. Originally HMOs were distinct from other insurance firms because providers were not paid on a fee-for-service basis and because enrollees faced no cost-sharing requirements. These distinctions no longer hold.

Everyone
Knows

Exceptional Hospitals

Three hospitals have been cited by Robert Levering and Milton Moskowitz in their book *The Hundred Best Companies to Work for in America* as exceptional places to work. They are Beth Israel Hospital of Boston, Baptist Hospital of Miami, and Methodist Hospital of Houston. What makes them so special? They stand out in five key areas:

- There is more employee participation in the decision-making process, especially around reorganizations.

- These institutions display more sensitivity to the problems of working parents, including such benefits as childcare benefits and flexible work schedules.

- More sharing of the wealth can be seen in these organizations. Profit-sharing and gain-sharing (where workers share in the risk-taking that may raise productivity and then are compensated when it is successful) programs are common.

- Employees who work for these institutions enjoy their work more and actually have the kind of fun that is not inconsistent with a serious, productive institution.

- There is more trust between management and employees, and it goes both ways. Indications of such trust are the absence of time clocks, regular meetings to discuss concerns, posting open positions on internal Web sites, and developmental opportunities.

Health Savings Account (HSA)   Enacted as part of the Medicare Modernization Act, people are permitted to have a high-deductible insurance plan along with a savings account to use toward health care expenses.

health systems   Also called integrated systems, these are multihospital systems with a range of outpatient services that allow for more coordinated patient care. Group practices, laboratories, and ambulatory care facilities are typically included. Individual hospitals, physicians and other medical facilities form a network to share quality standards, information, expertise, and technology that is difficult to provide alone. This not only helps to reduce the cost of care, but also helps to save lives. A successfully integrated system provides the best care for patients because all parts of the patient's needs are coordinated, including needs that come up between hospitalizations or other health services.

human resource management (HRM)   The role and responsibility of human resource managers in attracting, developing, and maintaining a suitable workforce to support the organizational goals.

incremental cost   Change in cost due to a change in production output.

Independent Practice Association (IPA)   A contracting organization for physicians made up of solo and small groups that enables them to contract with payers on a unified basis.

individual mandate   A proposed national health insurance plan under which individuals are required to buy a specified minimum level of health insurance.

infant mortality rate   The number of infant deaths in a year divided by the number of live births.

Integrated Delivery System (IDS)   A health care delivery system that includes or contracts with all of the health care providers for coordinated medical services to the patient.

interpersonal skills   Characteristics possessed by an individual that facilitate smooth interaction between that person and other people in a job setting.

job description   Used by human resources for hiring purposes, it is a list of the general tasks, functions, and responsibilities of a position. Typically it also includes information about qualifications needed, salary range, job hierarchy, and to whom the potential employee would report.

Joint Commission on Accreditation of Healthcare Organizations (JCAHO)   Begun in the 1950s to standardize the quality of care in hospitals, the Joint Commission now accredits and certifies more than 16,000 health care organizations and programs that include hospitals, long-term care facilities, psychiatric facilities, substance abuse programs, community mental health programs, ambulatory facilities, and hospices. Joint Commission accreditation and certification is recognized nationwide as a symbol of quality that reflects an organization's commitment to meeting certain performance standards.

just-in-time scheduling (JIT)   A way to reduce costs and improve workflow by scheduling items to arrive just in time to be used.

labor unions   These represent workers in many industries. Labor unions engage in collective bargaining over wages, benefits, and working conditions for their membership and represent their members if management attempts to violate contract provisions. Many hospital workers are members of unions.

leadership   Influencing others to do what needs to be done, especially those things that the leader believes should be accomplished.

malpractice   Negligence or carelessness of a professional person that results in injury or loss to a patient or client.

managed care organization (MCO)   This is an organization that controls medical care costs and quality through provider price discounts, utilization management, drug formularies, and profiling participating providers.

management   Organization and coordination of the activities of an enterprise in accordance with certain policies and in achievement of clearly defined objectives.

materials management   Sometimes called supply chain management, it is the process of managing the clinical and non-clinical goods and inventory purchased and used by the personnel of a health care organizations.

Medicaid   A health insurance program financed by federal and state governments and administered by states for low-income users.

Medical Care Price Index   Calculated by the Bureau of Labor Statistics and included as part of the Consumer Price Index to measure the rate of inflation in medical care prices.

medical coding   The process of transforming descriptions of medical diagnoses and procedures into universal medical code numbers. The diagnoses and procedures are usually taken from a variety of sources within the medical record, such as the transcription of the doctor's notes, laboratory results, radiologic results, and other sources.

Medicare   A federally sponsored health insurance plan for the elderly and disabled run by the Health Care Financing Administration.

On the Cutting
Edge

Physicians for a National Health Program

How do physicians feel about the overhaul of the health care system and the methods of disbursement being completely altered? One organization, Physicians for a National Health Program (PNHP), takes the counterintuitive approach and supports the single-payer option. In fact, the issue is the only one of the several options for national health insurance for which this group advocates—and they have been doing so since 1987. Why choose singe-payer over the other options? The group's Web site states that they oppose for-profit control or corporate control of the health system and favor single-payer financing. In service of this ideal, they educate physicians, other health workers, and the general public on the need for a comprehensive, high-quality, publicly funded health care program, accessible to all residents of the United States. They also believe in removing barriers to health care faced by the uninsured, the poor, minorities, and the undocumented. Their goal is to restore what it views as the primary mission of physicians—to act as professional advocates for patients.

Medicare Advantage plans   Enacted as part of the Medicare Modernization Act, private health plans receive a monthly capitation payment from Medicare and accept full financial risk for the cost of benefits.

mission statement   A statement from an organization that states its purpose, who it serves, and what it provides. Here is a sample mission statement from Sibley Hospital in Washington, D.C.: "The mission of Sibley Memorial Hospital is to provide quality health services and facilities for the community, to promote wellness, to relieve suffering, and to restore health as swiftly, safely, and humanely as it can be done, consistent with the best service we can give at the highest value for all concerned" (http://www.missionstatements.com).

multihospital system   When a corporation owns, leases, or manages two or more acute care hospitals.

Best
Practice

The New Rules for Leadership

Deedra Hartung of Cejka Search says that the new "hot" leadership skills for health care managers in the 21st century are:

- *High-level technological decision-process leadership skills.* Health care managers will have to ask the right questions and assess the technology thoroughly before selecting appropriate systems. In order to stay competitive, decisions have to be made accurately and rapidly.

- *Clinical connectivity.* That is, managers will have to include physician's perspectives to an even greater degree in business decisions. Many health care CEOs cite an effective physician relationship as among the top three core competencies for leaders.

- *Leading diverse management teams.* Even beyond racial, cultural, and gender diversity, health care leaders will also have to manage staff from diverse professional and educational backgrounds, with varying levels of expertise and knowledge bases. The manager should welcome and benefit from the diversity of viewpoints.

- *Fostering innovative thinking and problem-solving.* An innovative culture encourages formation of proactive solutions, services, and processes and it rewards risk-taking and proactive thinking. The visionary leader encourages a culture of innovation throughout the organization.

Myers-Briggs Type Indicator (MBTI)   A psychometric questionnaire designed to measure psychological preferences in how people perceive the world and make decisions.

National Practitioner Data Bank (NPDB)   A system whereby state licensing boards and other health care regulatory bodies can identify, discipline, and report those who engage in unprofessional behavior. The intent is to prevent incompetent health care professionals from moving from state to state without disclosure of past malpractice or adverse action history being known.

networking   A supportive system of sharing information and services among individuals and groups having a common interest.

nonmaleficence   Not increasing patients' difficulties by the actions or inactions of health care administrators and managers. The minimization of risk to patients is of primary importance, and health care managers are charged with protecting against intentional harm.

nonprice hospital competition   Hospitals compete on the basis of their facilities, services, and technology rather than on price.

nurse participation rate   The percentage of trained nurses who are employed at any health care facility like a hospital, ambulatory care center, group practice, or long-term care facility.

Occupational Safety and Health Act (OSHA)   Passed in 1970, OSHA requires employers to maintain a safe workplace and adhere to standards specific to health care employees.

open-enrollment period   A period of time, which can be a few months to a year, during which employees are given the option of enrolling in one or more health care plans.

operations management   Design, execution, and control of an organization's operations that convert its resources into desired goods and services and follows through by implementing its business strategy.

organization development (OD)   Planned and systematic process in which behavioral science principles and practices are used to improve organizational functioning.

out-of-pocket   The amount of money that a consumer directly pays for a good or service. In the case of health insurance, it is the amount the consumer pays after monies are reimbursed to the providers.

over-the-counter drug   A drug that is available without a prescription.

patient days   Total number of inpatient days of care given in a specified time period.

patient dumping   When a health care facility refuses to admit or prematurely discharges patients without resources or patients that require high cost procedures.

pay for performance   Higher payments made to providers who demonstrate that they provide higher-quality services.

peer review organization (PRO)   A watchdog group formed by members of the same profession to guard against improper

Professional
Ethics

Common Ethics

The American College of Healthcare Executives (ACHE)
Code of Ethics expresses ethical responsibilities of health
care leaders according to constituencies in the following
table:

Responsible Area	Guidelines
To the profession	Uphold the Code of Ethics
	Conduct professional activities with good faith, honesty, integrity, and respect
	Comply with all laws and regulations
	Implement a personal program of assessment and continuing professional education
	Avoid improper exploitation of professional relationships for personal gain
	Disclose conflicts of interest
	Respect professional confidences
	Refrain from any activity that demeans the health care management profession
To the patient	Evaluate the quality of care
	Avoid practicing discrimination
	Advise patients of rights, opportunities, responsibilities, and risks
	Facilitate conflict resolution
	Do not tolerate abuses of power
	Ensure confidentiality

treatment or charges. Sometimes PROs are used to review
questionable claims.

performance appraisal (PA)   A face-to-face discussion in which
one employee's job performance is discussed, appraised, and
reviewed by another using an agreed-upon set of criteria.

Responsible Area	Guidelines
To the organization	Provide health care within the bounds of available resources
	Improve community health care services
	Be truthful in all forms of organizational communication
	Prevent fraud and abuse and aggressive accounting practices that result in disputable financial reports
	Create an organizational environment where both clinical and management mistakes are minimized
	Provide ethics resources to staff
To employees	Provide a work environment that discourages harassment, coercion, and discrimination
	Provide a work environment that promotes proper use of employees knowledge and skills
	Establish appropriate grievance mechanisms
To the community	Participate in public dialogue on health care policy issues and advocate solutions that will improve health status
	Work to support health care access to all people
	Provide prospective patients with accurate information enabling them to make enlightened decisions regarding services

pharmacy benefit manager (PBM)   A firm that processes outpatient prescription drug claims for health insurer's drug plans.

physician agency relationship   When the physician acts on behalf of the patient.

physician hospital organization (PHO) An organization that allows hospitals and their medical staffs to develop group practice arrangements that facilitate negotiation of contracts.

planned change When a gap in performance is evident, a leader provides a plan for altering and improving the situation.

play or pay A form of national health insurance in which employers are required to provide a basic level of medical insurance to employees.

preferred provider organization (PPO) An arrangement between a panel of health care providers and purchasers of health care services in which the providers agree to supply services to a defined group at a discount.

primary care physician One who coordinates all of the routine medical care of an individual.

productivity Relative measure of the efficiency of a person, machine, factory, or system in converting inputs into useful outputs.

professional standards review organizations (PSROs) Formed to protect Medicare funds from fraud and abuse, PSROs are physician-run organizations that have the authority to grant or deny payments for Medicare and Medicaid services.

prospective payment system (PPS) A method of payment in which health care providers are paid a predetermined rate for the services rendered regardless of actual costs incurred.

providers A generic term for doctors, hospitals, nurses, dentists, therapists, and other who provide health care services.

rate review Review by a government or private agency of a hospital's budget and financial data, performed for the purpose of determining the reasonableness of the hospital rates and evaluating proposed rate increases.

refundable tax credit One of the proposals for national health insurance in which individuals are give a tax credit to purchase health insurance.

risk averse A characteristic in which the decision-maker is willing to accept an option with a lower expected value if it has less variability.

risk pool A population group that is defined by its expected claim experience.

second opinion When decisions to initiate a medical intervention are reviewed by two physicians.

self-directed team   Self-organized semi-autonomous small group whose members determine, plan, and manage their day-to-day activities and duties.

self-insurance   The method of providing employee benefits in which the group eligible for insurance purchases no insurance at all, thereby assuming full responsibility for the claims.

single payer   When a third party, usually the government, pays health care providers and the population has a choice of doctors, hospitals, and other providers. It is usually funded by taxation. Medicare and Medicaid are single-payer systems.

six sigma   A management strategy designed to improve the quality of outputs by identifying and removing the causes of defects and variation. It uses statistical methods and follows a defined sequence of steps.

skilled nursing facility   A long-term care facility that provides inpatient skilled care and rehabilitation services.

specialty health maintenance organization (Specialty HMO)   An organization that uses an HMO model to provide health care services in a subset or single specialty of medical care.

staff-model HMO   An HMO that directly employs staff physicians to provide services.

stakeholders   People or organizations who are interested in the health care facility, in this case, in terms of its operations and success. A stakeholder would be members of the boards of hospitals, community organizations that support clinics, and so forth.

SWOT analysis   A strategic planning method used to evaluate the **S**trengths, **W**eaknesses, **O**pportunities, and **T**hreats involved in a project or in a business.

team-building   Participation in a wide range of activities—like bonding exercises, retreats, and structured events—in order for an organization to strengthen the effectiveness of a team.

telehealth, telemedicine, e-Health   The use of telecommunications, usually from a distant site, to facilitate medical diagnoses, patient care, patient education, and/or medical learning. The communication is between someone with the information—physician, technician, nurse—to the person who is in need of it like a physician, emergency medical technician, and so forth. Modes of telecommunication include Internet, radio, optical, or electromagnetic channels transmitting text, X-rays, photographic images, medical records, voice transmission, data, or video. Many rural areas are finding uses for telehealth and telemedicine in providing oncology, home health, ER, radiology, and psychiatry.

tertiary care   Includes the most complex services in hospital settings, such as transplantations and open-heart surgery.

third-party administrator (TPA)   An organization such as an HMO, insurance company, or government agency that pays for all or part of the insured medical services.

tiers   To have lower costs, many prescription drug plans place drugs into different "tiers," which cost different amounts. Each plan can form their tiers in different ways. Here is an example of how a plan might form its tiers. One example may be: Tier 1 - Generic drugs, Tier 2 - Preferred brand-name drugs, Tier 3 - Non-preferred brand-name drugs.

unbundling   When a provider charges separately for services previously provided together as part of treatment.

uncompensated care   Services rendered by the provider without reimbursement.

underwriting   The process of assessing the risks associated with an insurance policy and setting the premium accordingly.

universal coverage   When the entire population is eligible for medical services.

upside-down pyramid   A way to look at the structure of a health care organization that puts the patients on the top of the pyramid, the workers in the middle, and the managers at the bottom. This structure puts the attention on the patients, with various levels of employees supporting them.

utilization management (UM)   The process of evaluating the necessity, appropriateness, and efficiency of health care services against established guidelines and criteria. UM usually includes new actions or decisions based on the overall analysis of the utilization.

variable costs   Costs that can vary with sales or output.

vertical integration   A delivery system that provides an entire range of services that includes inpatient care, ambulatory care clinics, outpatient surgery, and home care.

volume performance standards (VPS)   A mechanism to adjust updates to fee-for-service payment rates based on actual aggregates.

workers' compensation A state-mandated program providing insurance coverage for work-related injuries and disabilities. Several states have either enacted or are considering changes to the Workers Compensation Laws to allow employers to cover occupational injuries and illnesses within their own existing group medical plans. Some employers pay premiums to the state or to insurance companies for this coverage. Others are self-funded and use third party case management or administrative services to manage the processes.

workforce diversity Differences in ethnicity, age, race, gender, physical capability, religious affiliation, and sexual orientation among employees.

Resources

The theme running through this book is that the jobs in health care management are many and varied. Continuing that theme, you will find in this chapter listings of professional organizations, books and periodicals, and Web sites that will help you manage your career in health care management in the many settings in which they occur.

Associations and Professional Organizations

There are numerous professional associations related to health management, which can be subcategorized as either personal or institutional membership groups. Personal membership groups are joined by individuals, and typically have individual skill and career development as their focus. An example of one is the American Academy of Professional Coders. Institutional membership groups are joined by organizations; they typically focus on organizational effectiveness, and may also include data-sharing agreements and other best-practice sharing vehicles for member organizations. Prominent examples include the American Hospital Association and the University Health System Consortium. The organizations listed below are mostly of the individual type and represent the needs of all aspects of health care management occupations—marketing, finance, practice management, public relations, information technology, consultants, and more. Consult their Web sites for career information, policy initiatives, earnings surveys, and inside information.

Fast Facts

Turnover Rates

In 2006, Medical Group Management Association (MGMA) reported on administrative turnover rates in group practices.

Rate of Turnover	1–10%	11–20%	21–30%	31% or more
		64.41%	21.47%	8.47%	5.65%

American Academy of Medical Administrators attempts to unite diverse specialties of the broad, multidisciplinary medical administration community. It aims to improve the quality of health care leadership through communication and the open exchange of information.   (http://www.aameda.org)

American Academy of Professional Coders is the nation's largest medical coding training and certification organization. It prides itself on its ethical approaches to coding.   (http://www.aapc.com)

American Association of Healthcare Administrative Management provides education, certification, and advocacy for health care administrators.   (http://www.aaham.org)

American Association of Healthcare Consultants provides consulting services to the health care industry. They advise in several fields, including facilities planning, human resources, information technology, operations, physician practice management, and marketing, among others.   (http://www.aahc.net)

American Health Care Association advocates for quality care and services for the frail, elderly, and people with disabilities. Its members provide essential care to one million individuals in 11,000 nursing homes, assisted living facilities, and other long term care facilities.   (http://www.ahca.org)

American Health Planning Association seeks to improve community-based health service planning and decision-making. By

implementing practices that promote efficiency, equality, and security, it hopes to "provide a voice for the uninsured and the under-served in our communities." (http://www.ahpanet.org)

American Hospital Association is made up of over 5,000 hospitals, health care systems, networks, and other providers of care. In addition, it represents 37,000 individual members. It advocates for its member's concerns on the national level and in both the legislative and regulatory arenas. (http://www.aha.org)

American Public Health Association is the oldest org)anization of public health professionals in the world and has been working to improve public health since 1872. With its state affiliates, it represents over 50,000 health professionals and others who work to promote health throughout the nation. (http://www.apha.org)

Association of Hispanic Health Care Executives works to increase the number of Hispanic health care professionals in the United States. It seeks to improve access to health care in the Hispanic community as well as raise awareness of Hispanic health care needs. (http://www.ahhe.org)

Association of University Programs in Health Administration is a global network of colleges, universities, faculty, and organizations dedicated to raising the quality of health care through health care management education. It is the only non-profit organization of its kind. Its members come from more than 500 colleges and universities throughout the United States and Canada. (http://www.aupha.org)

Canadian Public Health Association is a national, independent, not-for-profit, voluntary association that works on behalf of public health in Canada while fostering relationships with the international public health community. (http://www.cpha.ca)

Healthcare Information Management Systems Society (HIMSS) is a health care–stakeholder membership org)anization focused on fine-tuning the use of information technology and management systems in the health care field. Founded in 1961 with offices in Chicago, Washington D.C., Brussels, Singapore, and other locations, HIMSS counts more than 23,000 individual members, over 380 corporate members, and nearly 30 not-for-profit organizations. (http://www.himss.org)

Hospice Foundation of America is the organizational home for hospice caretakers nationwide. Focusing on patients with terminal illnesses, caretakers place emphasis on pain relief and emotional counseling and connection. Described as "not a place but a

concept of care," roughly 80 percent of hospice assistance is given in patients' homes.   (http://www.hospicefoundation.org)

Institute for Diversity in Health Management works with health services org)anizations and educators to increase leadership opportunities for minorities in health services management. (http://www.diversityconnection.org)

Medical Transcription Industry Association looks to find new ways to integrate people with technology, thus improving clinical documentation solutions for health care delivery systems. (http://www.mtia.com)

National Association of Health Service Executives is a nonprofit association of black health care executives founded in 1968 for the purpose of promoting the advancement of black health care leaders. Through local and national initiatives, it seeks to improve quality and availability of health services as well as educational opportunities in the health care field.   (http://www.nahse.org)

National Association of Health Service Coordinators is dedicated to raising awareness of the need for well-educated health service coordinators in the health care industry. Falling somewhere between the duties of a nurse and a secretary, coordinators are responsible for keeping the wards of hospitals organized, transcribing physicians' notes, and providing general assistance to nurses and staff.   (http://www.nahuc.org)

National Center for Healthcare Leadership works to ensure that the health care sector is staffed with high-quality leaders. It places a special emphasis on researching the most effective ways of leadership, both inside and outside the health care field. (http://www.nchl.org)

National Rehabilitation Counseling Association was founded in 1958 to represent the concerns of rehabilitation counselors. Since then, the organization has grown to become the largest of its kind, representing rehabilitation counselors in all types of work environments.   (http://www.nrca-net.org)

Professional Association of Health Care Office Management is an organization devoted to nationalizing the health care office management workforce into a single, efficient communications network. It prides itself on rapid sharing of information and best practices, and aims to keep members up to date with the latest changes in medical rules and regulations.   (http://www.pahcom.com/about-pahcom.html)

On the Cutting Edge

The Personal Brand

Building a personal brand for health management professionals has become the latest trend. NAHSE, the nonprofit association of African-American health care managers, offers a way to start. The Young Healthcare Professionals Forum was developed to provide a rare networking opportunity for students and early careerists to gain valuable information from tenured health care professionals, build strong contacts with professionals representing a broad section of health care management, and share helpful insights with peers. By interacting with senior leaders in small group sessions at the annual meeting, early careerists deliberate on such topics as *The brand called you*, *Differentiating yourself from your colleagues*, and *How to customize your skills to reflect your personal brand*.

University HealthSystem Consortium, founded in 1984, is an alliance of 107 academic medical centers and 221 of their affiliated hospitals representing approximately 90 percent of the nation's non-profit academic medical centers.   (https://www.uhc.edu/home.htm)

Women Health Care Executives is an organization of women from all health care fields, who "come together to learn, support, inspire and encourage one another throughout their career." (http://www.whce.net)

Books and Periodicals

Think of the list of books and periodicals below as a "starter set" of essential books you would need on your shelf as a health care administrator. There are many more, of course, but the following list is a good place from which to build. The books cover the areas of career planning; health care administration and management, health care marketing, leadership, finance, business, policy, practice tools, and technology.

Books

Essentials of Health Care Marketing. By E.N. Berkowitz (Bartlett, 2006). This comprehensive text provides a foundational knowledge of the principles of marketing and their applications in health care. Moreover, as health care has changed over the past 20 years, it argues that the application of marketing principles also must shift to respond to the changing environmental forces of the marketplace.

Leadership in Health Care: Values at the Top. By Carson Dye (Administration Press, 2000). Carson Dye's ideas on leadership attributes for health care managers are based on long experience and thoughtful synthesis of that experience. His ideas are frequently referenced in this book. Dye points out that key values influence a health care leader's personal and professional behavior and drive effective leadership. He discusses the problems that leaders experience and then several chapters are devoted to the values that can be learned to confront those problems. Scenarios and self-evaluation questions are included as learning aids.

Health Policy Issues: An Economic Perspective (4th Ed.) By Paul Feldstein (Health Administration Press, 2007). You will confront policy issues in almost any role or setting. This book tackles the questions of physician shortages and surpluses, the pros and cons of the national health insurance plans being considered by Congress, the forces shaping the hospital's future role, and other issues. Full of charts and graphs, Dr. Feldstein lays out the issues so that they are easily understood.

Accounting Fundamentals for Healthcare Management. By Stephen A. Finkler & David M. Ward (Jones and Bartlett, 2006). For the accounting manager in a health care facility, this book focuses on basic accounting in health care management. It contains the vocabulary of and an introduction to the tools and concepts employed by finance officers. It will help anyone assess financial information, ask the appropriate questions, and understand the jargon-laden answers. This book is indispensable for anyone who manages a department and a budget in a health care setting.

Careers in Healthcare Management: How to Find Your Path and Follow It. By Cynthia C. Haddock, Robert A. McLean, & Robert C. Chapman (Health Administration Press, 2002). As experienced health care management professionals and academicians, the authors provide invaluable information about where you can work, the type of management positions available, and the skills you will need to be successful. Suggestions are offered for finding and using a mentor, pursuing graduate or continuing education, and honing management skills. The book contains 51 profiles of health care managers who, in their own words, describe how they prepared for their careers, what challenges they have encountered, and what advice they would provide for new managers.

A Career Guide for the Health Services Manager. By Anthony Kovner & Alan Channing (Health Administration Press, 1999). In this book you will learn where health services managers work, how to build an ideal career, what skills make a good manager, how to manage stakeholders and employees, and how to advance within an organization and within the industry. The authors, both highly experienced in the field, tell it like it is in accessible language.

Health Care Management: Tools and Techniques for Managing in a Health Care Environment. By Donald Lombardi & John R. Schermerhorn (Wiley, 2007). The authors use the CASE (content, analysis, synthesis, and evaluation) learning system to convey key health care management topics. There are numerous learning aids and assessment tools that help you learn the fundamental health care management concepts and to master the core competencies to succeed in the field. The chapters are comprehensive in their coverage of the important topics such as the fundamentals of organizational structures, legal and labor issues, planning tools and techniques, effective leadership, and much more.

Managing Technological Change: Organizational Aspects of Health Informatics (2nd Ed.) By Nancy Lorenzi & Robert Riley (Springer, 2003). Technology surrounds the health care manager, no matter where they work. In this book, the focus is on the organizational and interpersonal aspects of managing technological changes in health care systems. By emphasizing the role of human responses to change, the authors point out the skills necessary to manage new technological introductions.

From Management to Leadership: Practical Strategies for Health Care Leaders (2nd Ed.). By Jo Manion (Wiley, 2005). Health care consultant Jo Manion writes about the important interpersonal skills needed for effective leadership. She maintains that interpersonal skills are critical success factors that have not been examined adequately in a leadership context. The book identifies the fundamental interpersonal competencies every leader needs, provides suggestions for improving these skills, and gives examples for practice in health care leadership contexts.

Mastering Patient Flow: Using Lean Thinking to Improve Your Practice Operations. By Elizabeth Woodcock (MGMA, 2007). This book advertises itself as a completely updated and comprehensive manual on practice operations. Delivering the newest trends for practice efficiency, it focuses on centering workflow around the patient. Easily readable, the book delivers sound and timely techniques for reducing patient cycle time, streamlining scheduling methods, managing telephones, maximizing space capacity and utilization, and controlling costs. It also includes proven tools for benchmarking, creating action plans, and self-assessment, along with worksheets, tips, and case studies.

Journals and Professional Magazines

Journals and magazines are good places to get the latest information about what is going on in the field. The list below includes literature that informs several constituencies within the field, and some are associated with specific professional organizations.

AHANews is a daily compendium of stories from all across the nation that deal with health care and related fields. (http://AHAnews.com)

American Journal of Health Promotion seeks to close the distance between the theory and practice of health promotion by fostering discussion among the many disciplines involved in the field. (http://www.healthpromotionjournal.com)

American Journal of Public Health publishes original work in research, research methods, and program evaluation in the field

Best Practice

Pros and Cons of the Business Model

Emily Friedman, a health care analyst, says that running a health care facility like a business is both good and bad. In the *NCHL* newsletter, she states, "Although it needs to operate in a businesslike manner, health care is not a regular business. Tomorrow's leaders must be trained to follow business and competitive models where they apply, and only where they do no harm".

of public health. Its mission is to provide a forum for the advancement of public health research, as well as help shape public policy and educational standards.   (http://ajph.org)

CMA Today focuses on the needs, interests, and working environments of certified medical assistants nationwide. It keeps its readership aware of current trends in the field by providing in-depth coverage of new technologies and other developments.   (http://www.aama-ntl.org/CMAToday/about.aspx)

Health Affairs is described as "the leading journal of health policy thought and research." A peer-reviewed journal since 1981, it delves into issues of health care and healthcare policy with both a national and international focus.   (http://content.healthaffairs.org)

Health Data Management explores the intersection of information technology and health care. It prides itself on being written "exclusively by a team of experienced journalists" and has won several awards for its exceptional writing and reportage.   (http://www.healthdatamanagement.com)

Hospitals & Health Networks is the flagship publication of the American Hospital Association. It is geared primarily towards hospital executives, though workers in all areas of the field will find it worthwhile reading.   (http://www.hhnmag.com)

Marketing Healthcare Today covers all aspects of healthcare marketing, from advertising campaigns to specific promotional materials, and looks "to rekindle creative inspiration" in its readers.   (http://www.mhtmagazine.com/contact.php)

Modern Healthcare features breaking news in the field of healthcare. The online version of this very popular journal is updated daily with news and commentary.   (http://www.modernhealthcare.com)

Perspectives in Health Information Management is the scholarly journal of the AHIMA Foundation. Since 2004, this peer-reviewed publication has helped improve health information management systems and methods via interdisciplinary dialogue.   (http://www.ahima.org/perspectives)

Web Sites

Web sites for professional organizations, journals, and educational institutions are included above in their respective sections. Below, you will find career Web sites for health care administration and general sites about the field that are not included above.

American Hospital Directory provides databases for any hospital nationwide. Profiles include key characteristics, utilization, and financial information. If you are looking for a hospital job, search this site for information about characteristics of the institution that you are interested in.   (http://www.ahd.com)

Bureau of Labor Statistics, Department of Labor site will tell you all you need to know about earnings, job outlook, related information, and links to other relevant sites. Check it out for information on geographic density of certain jobs and where the need is greatest.   (http://www.bls.gov/oco/ocos014.htm)

Cejka Search is a leading health care executive search firm. The site lists health care management jobs plus it provides information on career planning, compensation, contract negotiation, and it has a useful library that contains articles of interest for the health care manager.   (http://executivejobs.cejkasearch.com)

Health Leaders Media is a media site for health leaders that provides information on aspects of health subjects through a variety of media. (http://www.healthleadersmedia.com)

Health Resources and Services Administration of the U.S. Department of Health & Human Services is where you can find information about the latest in legislation, policy, and trends in employment. One part of the site directs you to the health care jobs that are in greatest demand.   (http://www.hrsa.gov)

The big advantage to the **National Association of Advisors for the Health Professions** site is the advisor network for those looking for advice on careers and on working day to day. Though the site looks like it concentrates on advising for clinical jobs, advisors are available in the four quadrants of the United States to provide advice on health management careers as well.   (http://www.naahp.org)

Pam Pohly's Internet Guide to management resources for medical and health care professionals will amaze you with its wealth of up-to-date articles, information, reference materials, and links available for your career enhancement and professional development.   (http://www.pohly.com/index.html)

Index